Deliver Us from Evil

The Didsbury Lectures

Series Preface

The Didsbury Lectures, delivered annually at Nazarene Theological College, Manchester, are a well-established feature on the theological calendar in Britain. Through being available live, online, and by their publication, the lectures have reached a global audience.

The name "Didsbury Lectures" has a double significance: Didsbury is the location of Nazarene Theological College, and it was the location of Didsbury College, established in 1842 for training Wesleyan Methodist ministers.

In 1979, the Didsbury Lectures were inaugurated by Professor F. F. Bruce. He has been followed annually by highly regarded scholars, such as Thomas F. Torrance and N. T. Wright, who established the series' standard. The lectures give a platform for leading thinkers within the historic Christian faith to address topics of current relevance that traditionally would fall into the category of "divinity."

From the start, the college envisaged the series as a means of contributing to theological discourse between the church and the academic community. Publication is an important part of fulfilling that goal. It is the hope and prayer of the College that each volume will have a positive and lasting impact on scholarship and in the life of the church in its witness to the gospel of Christ.

1979	Professor F. F. Bruce†	*Men and Movements in the Primitive Church*
1980	The Revd Professor I. Howard Marshall †	*Last Supper and Lord's Supper*
1981	The Revd Professor James Atkinson†	*Martin Luther: Prophet to the Church Catholic*
1982	The Very Revd Professor T. F. Torrance†	*The Mediation of Christ*
1983	The Revd Professor C. K. Barrett†	*Church, Ministry and Sacraments in the New Testament*
1984	The Revd Dr A. R. G. Deasley	*The Shape of Qumran Theology*
1985	Dr Donald P. Guthrie†	*The Relevance of John's Apocalypse*
1986	Professor Andrew F. Walls	The Nineteenth-Century Missionary Movement
1987	The Revd Dr A. Skevington Wood†	*Reason and Revelation*
1988	The Revd Professor Morna D. Hooker	*Not Ashamed of the Gospel: New Testament Interpretations of the Death of Christ*
1989	The Revd Professor Ronald E. Clements	*Wisdom in Theology*
1990	The Revd Professor Colin E. Gunton†	*Christ and Creation*
1991	The Revd Professor J. D. G. Dunn	*Christian Liberty: A New Testament Perspective*
1992	The Revd Dr Paul M. Bassett	The Spanish Inquisition
1993	Professor David J. A. Clines	*The Bible in the Modern World*

1994	The Revd Professor James B. Torrance†	*Worship, Community, and the Triune God of Grace*
1995	The Revd Dr R. T. France†	*Women in the Church's Ministry*
1996	Professor Richard Bauckham	*God Crucified: Monotheism and Christology in the New Testament*
1997	Professor H. G. M. Williamson	*Variations on a Theme: King, Messiah and Servant in the Book of Isaiah*
1998	Professor David Bebbington	*Holiness in Nineteenth Century England*
1999	Professor L. W. Hurtado	*At the Origins of Christian Worship*
2000	Professor Clark Pinnock†	*The Most Moved Mover: A Theology of God's Openness*
2001	Professor Robert P. Gordon	*Holy Land, Holy City: Sacred Geography and the Interpretation of the Bible*
2002	The Revd Dr Herbert McGonigle†	*John Wesley*
2003	Professor David F. Wright†	*What Has Infant Baptism Done to Baptism? An Enquiry at the End of Christendom*
2004	The Very Revd Dr Stephen S. Smalley	*Hope for Ever: The Christian View of Life and Death*
2005	The Rt Revd Professor N. T. Wright	*Surprised by Hope*
2006	Professor Alan P. F. Sell†	*Nonconformist Theology in the Twentieth Century*
2007	Dr Elaine Storkey	Sin and Social Relations
2008	Dr Kent E. Brower	*Living as God's Holy People: Holiness and Community in Paul*
2009	Professor Alan Torrance	Religion, Naturalism, and the Triune God: Confronting Scylla and Charybdis
2010	Professor George Brooke	The Dead Sea Scrolls and Christians Today
2011	Professor Nigel Biggar	*Between Kin and Cosmopolis: An Ethic of the Nation*
2012	Dr Thomas A. Noble	*Holy Trinity: Holy People: The Theology of Christian Perfecting*
2013	Professor Gordon Wenham	*Rethinking Genesis 1–11*
2014	Professor Frances Young	*Construing the Cross: Type, Sign, Symbol, Word, Action*
2015	Professor Elaine Graham	*Apologetics without Apology*
2016	Professor Michael J. Gorman	*Missional Theosis in the Gospel of John*
2017	Professor Philip Alexander & Professor Loveday Alexander	Priesthood and Sacrifice in the Epistle to the Hebrews
2018	Professor Markus Bockmuehl	The Four Evangelists on the Presence and Absence of Jesus
2019	Professor Michael Lodahl	*Matthew Matters*
2020	Professor John Swinton	*Deliver Us from Evil*
2021	Professor John Barclay	Beyond Charity: Rethinking Gift and Community with Paul
2022	Professor David Wilkinson	How Does God Act in the World?
2023	Professor Amos Yong	
2024	Professor John Behr	

Deliver Us from Evil

A Call for Christians to Take Evil Seriously

THE DIDSBURY LECTURES

JOHN SWINTON

CASCADE *Books* • Eugene, Oregon

DELIVER US FROM EVIL
A Call for Christians to Take Evil Seriously

The Didsbury Lectures Series

Cascade Books
An Imprint of Wipf and Stock Publishers
199 W. 8th Ave., Suite 3
Eugene, OR 97401

www.wipfandstock.com

PAPERBACK ISBN: 978-1-6667-3400-3
HARDCOVER ISBN: 978-1-6667-2939-9
EBOOK ISBN: 978-1-6667-2940-5

Cataloguing-in-Publication data:

Names: Swinton, John, 1957– [author]

Title: Deliver us from evil : a call for Christians to take evil seriously / by John Swinton.

Description: Eugene, OR: Cascade Books, 2022 | The Didsbury Lectures Series | Includes bibliographical references and index.

Identifiers: ISBN 978-1-6667-3400-3 (paperback) | ISBN 978-1-6667-2939-9 (hardcover) | ISBN 978-1-6667-2940-5 (ebook)

Subjects: LCSH: Good and evil—Religious aspects—Christianity | Theodicy | Theology, Practical | Genocide—Rwanda | COVID-19 Pandemic, 2020–

Classification: BT160 S95 2022 (print) | BT160 (ebook)

11/08/22

Contents

Acknowledgements

As with all books there are many people that I need to thank. The chapters of this book emerged from a series of lectures I presented as the Didsbury Lectures at the Nazarene College in Manchester, England in 2020. Due to the pandemic they had to be done online which turned out quite well as it meant that people who wouldn't have been able to attend normally could do so virtually. I'm grateful for the thoughts, comments, and challenges that people brought to me in that context. Thank you to those colleagues and friends who took the time to read through this book and gave me some invaluable thoughts and feedback. I'm grateful to my co-worker in practical theology at Aberdeen, Katie Cross, as well as Susan Eastman at Duke Divinity School, North Carolina, whose thinking is an important dimension of this book. I am also thankful to my friend and colleague Ulrike Guthrie for her invaluable editorial advice. Thanks are due also to Beverley Gaventa, Medi Volpe, Philip Ziegler, and Emmanuel Katongole, who have all helped along the road. Many thanks to Rob Heimburger for his very thoughtful reflections on the text and for his excellent work on the index for this book. Writing about evil is always a challenge, so thanks are due to all of those who prayed for me and with me along the way. It's been a journey.

Introduction

"Deliver Us from Evil . . ."

Evil

The killing of George Floyd

On May 25, 2020, George Floyd, a forty-six-year-old African American, was murdered by Derek Chauvin, a white policeman in the US city of Minneapolis. Chauvin knelt on Floyd's neck for nine minutes and twenty-nine seconds while Floyd was handcuffed and lay face down in the street. The murder itself was horrific enough. But what was equally as concerning was the action of the other officers, or rather, the *inaction* of the other officers. They simply stood around and watched. There was no desire to intervene and indeed one of the officers actively prevented bystanders from intervening. *How could it be that someone could stand and watch a murder, and think that nothing wrong is going on?*

The persecution of Christians

> A woman in India watches as her sister is dragged off by Hindu nationalists. She doesn't know if her sister is alive or dead. A man in a North Korean prison camp is shaken awake after being beaten unconscious; the beatings

> begin again. A woman in Nigeria runs for her life. She has escaped from Boko Haram, who kidnapped her. She is pregnant, and when she returns home, her community will reject her and her baby. A group of children are laughing and talking as they come down to their church's sanctuary after eating together. Instantly, many of them are killed by a bomb blast. It's Easter Sunday in Sri Lanka.[1]

These people come from different countries, but they share one commonality. They are Christians and they are being persecuted for their faith. *How can it be that over forty million Christians live in places where there are high levels of persecution, and all of our churches are not outraged and spurred on to unceasing prayer and action?*

Children are dying. Does anyone care?

The World Health Organization estimates that in 2019 5.2 million children under the age of five died from preventable and treatable causes. Children aged one to eleven months accounted for 1.5 million of these deaths with children aged one to four accounting for 1.3 million deaths. Newly born children make up the remaining 2.4 million deaths.[2] In addition to this, half a million children aged from five to nine died in 2019:

> Leading causes of death in children under-5 years are preterm birth complications, birth asphyxia/trauma, pneumonia, congenital anomalies, diarrhoea and malaria, all of which can be prevented or treated with access to simple, affordable interventions including immunization, adequate nutrition, safe water and food and quality care by a trained health provider when needed.[3]

1. Open Doors, "Christian Persecution." https://www.opendoorsusa.org/christian-persecution/ (accessed February 9, 2022).

2. World Health Organization, "Children: Improving Survival and Well-Being." https://www.who.int/news-room/fact-sheets/detail/children-reducing-mortality (accessed January 24, 2022).

3. World Health Organization, "Children: Improving Survival and Well-being."

Why might it be that we are not outraged and driven to action by such statistics. How can we know such a thing and simply go on living our lives as if the deaths of millions meant little to us?

These are big questions that tell us something important about the nature of evil. It's not always what you might think it is and it's not always easy for people to see it. This book is about learning to see and resist evil, particularly in those spaces within creation where it may not at first be obvious. When we *see* evil, we can resist it. If evil remains invisible, it will consume us.

The Outline of the Book

In chapter 1, I explore the nature of evil. Here I bring together two key thinkers—Susan Eastman and Hannah Arendt—who, whilst coming from quite different disciplines and perspectives, come to remarkably similar conclusions about the nature of evil. New Testament scholar Susan Eastman explores the way in which sin and evil are described in Paul's letter to the Romans. Paul's thinking locates evil and sin within the cognitive confusion that human beings experience when they move away from God and confuse themselves and their own perspectives with the things of God. Evil occurs when people begin to mistake good for bad, right for wrong, and the things of God for the things that human beings desire. Evil is a form of cognitive dissonance that stems from alienation from God but manifests itself in actions and views that alienate us from one another, and that ultimately lead to violence and disruption. Eastman points out that evil and sin are not necessarily the same thing for Paul. Evil is something that people do. Sin is a power that lords it over human beings. Only the death and resurrection of Jesus can ultimately redeem human beings from the power of sin. In the interim we are called to notice and resist the evil that surrounds us.

Hannah Arendt's thinking on evil has an unusual resonance with Eastman's analysis of Paul. For Arendt, evil can be radical, but it can also be banal. Banal evil occurs when we simply fail to think about certain things and in so doing find ourselves implicated in evil even though we may not notice it. In Arendt, once again, we find a kind of cognitive dissonance that leads to us not noticing evil in the apparent innocence of day-to-day attitudes and ways of thinking.

In chapter 2, I will pick up on a contemporary example of Arendt's idea of the banality of evil, and show some of the ways in which evil manifested itself in relation to the 2020 COVID-19 pandemic. Evil likes to hide and confuse. The pandemic is a perfect opportunity for evil to flourish. However, the flourishing of evil during the pandemic is not necessarily obvious. Instead of using arguments relating to theodicy to try to explain the pandemic, in this chapter I consider the ways in which evil hides and reveals itself in unusual places in the midst of the suffering and uncertainly of a pandemic, the issue being not *why* there is evil, but *what we can do about it when we discover it.*

In chapter 3 I turn my attention to the subject of radical evil. Evil can certainly manifest itself within the banality of everyday life, but that is not the only way in which it reveals itself. In this chapter I return to the problematic tension in Arendt's work between banal and radical evil. I do this through a theological exploration of the genocide that occurred in Rwanda in 1994. The twentieth century has been a century of genocides. These have occurred in various places such as Bosnia-Herzegovina, Cambodia, Nazi Germany, Stalin's Russia, and Turkey, to name but a few. While all these atrocities should draw theological attention, the Rwandan genocide is particularly disturbing as it was carried out by Christians on Christians in a country that was one of the most successfully missionized countries in Africa. The question of how Christians could behave in such ways is complex. Listening to the narratives of the killers, it is clear that God was put to one side in favor of the state until the job was done. Those Christians could have put on the armor of faith but instead chose to discard it entirely. Why?

In chapter 4 we begin to think about the issue of resistance. How can evil be resisted and ultimately overcome? My focus here is particularly on spiritual warfare and the role of worship in forming a people who can both see and resist evil. Here I begin to address the complex issues around evil and suffering that have been highlighted in the previous discussions, especially this question: how can we resist temptation and be delivered from evil in a world that struggles even to recognize some things as evil?

1

The Nature of Evil

The Priority of Good and Evil as an Absence

This chapter explores some ways of understanding and ultimately responding faithfully to the multifaceted reality of evil. I begin with the doctrine of creation, or more specifically, the doctrine of creation *out of nothing*. The systematic theologian Ian McFarland points out that there are two dimensions of the creation story that relate directly to our understanding of evil: that God created the world *out of nothing* (*creatio ex nihilo*), and that God said that the world was *good*. The fact that the world was created out of nothing rather than something is important for these current purposes, because "Creation from nothing means that God is the sole condition of the world's existence in every respect and at every moment."[1] There is no room here for Manichean forms of dualism, which see evil as a negative force or power that is somehow equal but opposite to God. There is only one creative force, and it is wholly good. Evil is certainly a reality,[2] but it is a reality

1. McFarland, "The Problem of Evil," 323.

2. There is a flexibility in the concept of "reality." We might distinguish

that emerges *after* God creates the world and proclaims creation to be good. It is therefore not a product of God's good creative intentions. It is a distortion of God's creation. *Evil is that which God does not desire.* McFarland names evil as those things within creation that are against God's will.

Evil is not an aspect of the goodness of creation. Yet neither is evil an independent force. Instead, it is a distortion of creation's goodness. Within creation, God ascribes each creature a place. We recognize God's goodness in God's desire for God's creatures to flourish—to achieve ways of living within creation that are in line with their God-given nature. Put slightly differently, God desires God's creatures to flourish *according to their nature.* Evil is "that which threatens or inhibits creatures' flourishing as the beings God intends them to be."[3] If the essential meaning of human flourishing is to love God, self, and neighbor, as Jesus indicates (Mark 12:31), then evil is all that stands against such love. Evil tempts people to perceive the world in ways that distort the things of God and avoid and disrupt relationships between God and humans, and humans with each other. Evil lurks within such things as false perceptions of the world, racial and cultural stereotypes, misrepresentations, cultural blindness, and depersonalizing misidentifications, such a sexism, disablism, and xenophobia. The acknowledgement of the love of God and the presence of love and human flourishing are

between that which is ontologically real and that which is non-ontologically real. Something has ontological reality if it has being and form—i.e., it is some *thing* in the world, like a tree or a football or a human person. But something can also be real in a different sense, not in the sense of being a thing, but *the absence of a thing.* A hole in the roof, for instance, is not a thing—it is, in a way, nothing, an absence not a presence. But it is "real" in some sense and it has real-world consequences (as our rain-drenched carpet might testify). This observation is important when, for example, we think about whether evil is *an ontological presence* or *an absence of goodness.* If it is a presence, it is real because is a positive thing and it actively does something. If it is an absence, even though it may not have ontological reality, in the sense that it is not a substance, it is very real in its consequences for things that do have ontological reality. So even evil understood in terms of an absence of the good rather than a physical presence has practical significance.

3. McFarland, *From Nothing*, 324.

two indicators that evil is being resisted. When these things are absent, we know evil is either with us, or on its way.

Why Does Evil Exist?

The question "why does evil exist?" is, as I have argued elsewhere, an unanswerable mystery.[4] *Creatio ex nihilo* emphasizes that evil is not God's intention (God is good). That God seems to permit evil is both mysterious and deeply frustrating for us. *That* God permits evil seems obvious. *Why* God permits evil we do not know. Yet Matthew's parable of the weeds gives us a fascinating insight:

> Jesus told them another parable: "The kingdom of heaven is like a man who sowed good seed in his field. But while everyone was sleeping, his enemy came and sowed weeds among the wheat, and went away. When the wheat sprouted and formed heads, then the weeds also appeared. The owner's servants came to him and said, 'Sir, didn't you sow good seed in your field? Where then did the weeds come from?' '*An enemy did this*,' he replied."[5]

"An *enemy* did this." That's chilling. It's the point in a Stephen King novel when you suddenly realize that what you thought was going on is quite different from what is *actually* going on; the person you trusted and wanted to triumph turns out not to be quite as she first appeared. There is a malignant presence that you hadn't accounted for . . . and it's already here! Precisely who or what the enemy is is not yet clear. What *is* clear, however, is that there seems to be a force at work within creation that is out of kilter with God's good plan, and which seeks to sow the seeds of human destruction. That force is active in the midst of the world. It is, however, a *defeated* force. The parable continues:

> The servants asked him, "Do you want us to go and pull them up?" "No," he answered, "because while you are pulling the weeds, you may uproot the wheat with them.

4. Swinton, *Raging with Compassion*.

5. Matt 13:24–28, emphasis added.

> Let both grow together until the harvest. At that time I will tell the harvesters: First collect the weeds and tie them in bundles to be burned; then gather the wheat and bring it into my barn." (Matt 13:28–30)

The idea that evil is interspersed with good seed is so empirically obvious that we might overlook it. But it is vitally important. Resisting evil will require that we develop the skills to discern evil in the apparent normality of our everyday lives. Without that discernment we risk harming the innocent. There is no justification for collateral damage in the Gospels. Fighting evil is subtle, careful, thoughtful, and powerful in its sensitivity. Wherever there is good there is probably evil. Working out which is which can be very difficult, as we shall see.

The complex and hidden nature of evil is not a reason for us to become resigned or complacent. The fact that this enemy will be with us until Jesus returns does not mean that we have to come to terms with the evil that it propagates. We don't let child abuse go undetected and unpunished in the hope that all will end well. To do such a thing would itself be a mode of evil: "If anyone causes one of these little ones—those who believe in me—to stumble, it would be better for them to have a large millstone hung around their neck and to be drowned in the depths of the sea" (Matt 18:6). Ignoring evil (or implicitly or explicitly covering it up), is one way of becoming implicit in evil. God calls us to be aware of the presence of evil and to resist the enemy at all times (1 Pet 5:8).

In summary, *Creatio ex nihilo* reminds us that:

- God created the world and declared it good. It is good but somehow broken.
- God did not create evil, nor does God intend evil for God's creatures.
- Evil is not an aspect of God's being. "God is love" (1 John 4:8). God is good and loving: "Every good and perfect gift is from above, coming down from the Father of the heavenly lights, who does not change like shifting shadows" (Jas 1:17).

- Evil is not an illusion.
- God is not powerless against evil, but for reasons that are hidden from us, God chooses not to destroy it completely yet.
- God is active in the world through human beings and through spiritual warfare to bring about God's desired ends.
- In the final judgment, God will defeat evil.
- For now, Christians are called to look out for and resist evil.

Having laid down this foundational perspective on creation and evil, we must now thicken it by turning to the work of the apostle Paul in the book of Romans. Here we will engage with New Testament scholar Susan Eastman and her reflections on sin and evil in Paul's letter to the Romans, alongside of the work of the German philosopher Hannah Arendt on banal and radical evil.

Evil and Sin in Paul

Distinguishing evil and sin

One of the big problems for us nowadays is truth. Fake news and lie telling have become normalized within the political arena. The internet provides us with a lot of information, but not necessarily a lot of wisdom, knowledge, and truth. Working out what is and is not true can be challenging! This uncertainty about truth is a perfect breeding ground for evil. The stories we believe determine the things that we see (and do not see). What we think we see (and what we do not see) profoundly influences our actions. When you have competing versions of "the truth" confusion reigns.

In her essay "The Empire of Illusion: Sin, Evil, and Good News in Romans," Susan Eastman[6] examines the nature of evil and sin in Paul's letter to the Romans. She reminds us that for Paul, *evil is the product of human action*. It is *something that people*

6. Susan Eastman, "Empire of Illusion: Sin, Evil, and Good News in Romans," in *Comfortable Words: Essays in Honour of Paul F. M. Zahl*, edited by John D. Koch and Todd H. Brewer (Eugene, OR: Pickwick 2013), 3–21.

do. Importantly, as will become clear, actions do not have to be evil in their intention—as murder, violence, etc., are—to result in evil. It is the *result* (product) of the action that is key. Put slightly different, actions with evil consequences are evil actions even if they were not intended to be. This of course makes human action complex, ambiguous, and unpredictable. *Sin*, on the other hand, is a force, a power that lies beyond the things that people do, even if it is worked out through human actions. These two things are obviously intertwined. According to Romans 7, evil is what sin does through human actions, and (at least sometimes) contrary to the human desire for the good. Nevertheless, recognizing the difference is important. Evil involves human action. Hitler, the Cambodian revolutionary Pol Pot, and the perpetrators of genocide in Rwanda were all human beings who made certain decisions that have psychological, social, political, and historical dimensions. At this level, certain causal explanations can be applied that help us to make some sense of the evil that was perpetrated. This does not excuse such behavior or take away the responsibility of those involved. It does indicate that an aspect of such evil lies in the choices, decisions, and ways of thinking in which human beings engage, and it also reminds us that such choices, ways of thinking, and cognitive orientations have complex roots. Acknowledging sin as a power transcending particular human actions reminds us that there is something else going on beyond human control, something more malignant, complex, and troublesome than mere human weakness. Chapter 4 explores such "powers." For now, it is important to note that evil is both explainable and unexplainable, resistible, and beyond our control.

Losing the language of evil

Eastman is concerned that the language of evil is losing its power within contemporary society. Disciplines such as psychology, psychiatry, and sociology have proposed other explanations for sin and evil, giving us an alternative language. It is not that these disciplines are unhelpful in understanding evil. The problem is that each tends to *reduce* the issue of evil to within its own frame of reference, often excluding the language of theology. For a theologically minded person, the difficulty is that such explanations locate the source of evil *solely within human beings*, whether in my self or other selves. Such disciplines perceive evil to be a free-floating, purely human-oriented concept, thus avoiding the significance of sin-as-a-power.

This purely human-focused understanding sets up the possibility for "righteous battles against evil," with evil being located firmly within *other* people. When George W. Bush talked about the axis of evil lying in North Korea, Iran, and Iraq, he was opening a space for holy war within which the "good" is called to battle against the "evil other." We are all aware of the ambiguity of the ensuing War on Terror: lies, distortions, and hatred ensue when we begin to attribute evil to those who oppose us and not to the larger web of evil (or *the powers*). This is what Desmond Tutu meant when he spoke of apartheid as an evil that enslaved not only the oppressed but also the oppressors.[7]

The power of distorted perceptions

Eastman challenges the idea that evil is located solely within the self and proposes instead that evil and sin are *personal*, *communal*, and *suprapersonal*. As his book's title suggests, in *The Death of Satan: How Americans Have Lost Their Sense of Evil* Andrew Delbanco concluded that: "The essential modern evasion was the failure to acknowledge evil, name it, and accept its irreducibility in the self."[8] Eastman recognizes Delbanco's cultural critique but she turns towards theology, arguing that for Paul the primary problem for human beings lies in their "failure to acknowledge *God*, name *God as God*, and accept that God cannot be reduced to the self."[9] This basic ability to discern the things of God is

7. Desmond Tutu, Nobel Lecture, December 11, 1984.

8. Delbanco, *The Death of Satan*, 197.

9. Eastman, "Empire of Illusion," 5.

fundamental for an accurate account of sin and evil and a faithful reading of the world. Otherwise, serious cognitive distortions and profound perceptual difficulties ensue. Evil and sin distort our perceptions and prevent us from discerning what is good from what is bad. If we end up thinking that the darkness within us is in fact light, we are in deep trouble:

> The eye is the lamp of the body. If your eyes are healthy, your whole body will be full of light. But if your eyes are unhealthy, your whole body will be full of darkness. If then the light within you is darkness, how great is that darkness! (Matt 6:22–23)

If we cannot see the world clearly and name it accurately, if we cannot see violence even when it is right in front of us, we cannot live and act faithfully within it. As Richard Rohr observes:

> Jesus was absolutely honest when he said, "Father, forgive them, they do not know what they are doing" (Luke 23:34). Most people live a largely unconscious life. Most evil is first done more out of blindness and ignorance than out of malice.[10]

This is why the apostle John is prescient in observing that, "They will put you out of the synagogue; in fact, the time is coming when anyone who kills you will think they are offering a service to God." He knew that good people do very bad things when they believe they are inhabiting the moral high ground.

When we become disoriented in relation to what is true and godly, we end up living in what Eastman (after Chris Hedges) calls an "Empire of Illusion."[11] It is impossible to escape from the Empire of Illusion because by definition it is illusory. We can now begin to see how and why police officers can stand around watching a murder and not see anything wrong going on. It's not that they are necessarily bad people. They are simply caught up within a system of power that makes the discernment of good

10. Rohr, *The World, the Flesh, and the Devil*, 72.

11. Hedges, *The Empire of Illusion: The Loss of Literacy and the Rise of Spectacle.*

and evil illusive. As we shall see in chapter 4, all of us are caught up in systems of power that distort our vision, and all of us can lose our awareness of the presence of evil.

Eastman argues that revealing this kind of illusion and offering a way of accurately perceiving the world and everything in it is fundamental to Paul's understanding of evil and sin and how to discern and resist it. In Romans 12:2, Paul writes: "Do not conform to the pattern of this world but be transformed by the renewing of your mind. Then you will be able to test and approve what God's will is—his good, pleasing, and perfect will." This verse is closely related to his perspective on evil and sin earlier in the book. In order to overcome the cognitive confusion brought about by evil and sin, we need the transforming power of Jesus. Only then can we begin to see accurately and think straight. What exactly do I mean by that?

Evil and sin

For Paul, sin and evil are interconnected but not synonymous. In the first three chapters of Romans, Paul emphasizes that evil is *something that humans do.* He depicts humans as having been handed over by God to an "unreasoning mind" and improper conduct, precisely because they did not "see fit" to acknowledge God (1:28–30).[12] Paul's picture of evil and evildoing relates to the enmeshment of human beings in webs of falsehood and violence, "accompanied by a corresponding suppression of human capacities for perception and cognition":[13] In Romans 1:21–25 Paul says:

> For although they knew God, they neither glorified him as God nor gave thanks to him, but their thinking became futile and their foolish hearts were darkened. Although they claimed to be wise, they became fools and exchanged the glory of the immortal God for images made to look like a mortal human being and birds and animals and reptiles. Therefore God gave them over in

12. Eastman, "Empire of Illusion," 6.

13. Eastman, "Empire of Illusion," 10.

> the sinful desires of their hearts to sexual impurity for the degrading of their bodies with one another. They exchanged the truth about God for a lie and worshipped and served created things rather than the Creator—who is for ever praised. Amen.

Recognizing how vital it is that we understand what evil *does*, Eastman notes that our:

> cognitive and perceptual impairment has important implications. It means that the difference between "truth" and "falsehood" is not located in the *intentions* of the individual, but in the difference between an accurate ("truthful") or distorted ("false") orientation to the fundamental reality of God's creation and rule in the cosmos. Deception thus goes deeper than consciously false speech; it concerns, rather, the idolatry that creates and maintains an alternative, counterfeit personal reality.[14]

When we start to talk about the only truth being *my* truth, or about truth being flexible—and "my version of truth differs from yours," we find ourselves taking the first steps towards being drawn into evil. Evil confuses us about what is good and what is bad; what is of God and what is of human desire. It stops us seeing and thinking accurately. Importantly, *we don't have to intend to be evil to do evil:* we just need to lose our sense of truth and falsehood. This is not simply a matter of choice. People are born into situations that constrain or/and distort perception. The issue here is not simply personal sin, but the presence of *systems of sin* that prevent people from seeing properly and in so doing inhibit and ultimately destroy the possibility of human flourishing. Sin seen as a power that is embedded in systems indicates a *corporate dimension* to the processes of evil which we overlook at our peril.

In illuminating and developing Eastman's points, it will be helpful to turn to the thinking of the German philosopher Hannah Arendt and her ideas on evil in general and the banality of evil in particular.

14. Eastman, "Empire of Illusion," 10–11.

Radical Evil

The inexplicability of evil

In her earlier work on totalitarianism (a system of government that is centralized and dictatorial and requires complete subservience to the state), Hannah Arendt developed the idea of *radical evil.*[15] Radical evil is demonic, dark, unimaginable. It is more than dehumanizing. It is designed to do away with the very concept of humanity. She argued that the kind of evil that emerged from Nazism and that was encountered in concentration camps such as Auschwitz is radical (or entrenched or root-like) in that it drives a stake into the very foundations of our humanness. There are no humanly comprehensible motives for doing the things that were done there. The radical evil of the concentration camps struck at the heart of the Kantian imperative always to treat people as an end in themselves. Such was not the treatment of the camps' victims. But it was worse than that. Kant said that it was always wrong to treat people as a means to an end, yet even that is better than what happened in the camps. If one treats someone as a means to an end, they are still considered to have some utility or value in helping one achieve some kind of goal. Radical evil sinks lower still. The radical evil of places like Auschwitz destroyed *all* possibility of meaning. People within the camps were not treated as means that brought about a particular end. People were treated as being *valueless:*

> concentration camp inmates are treated not as persons, nor even as things or means, worthy of achieving a particular end, but as intrinsically valueless, as completely useless and thus as totally superfluous.[16]

Radical evil destroys spontaneity and in so doing annihilates the very essence of humanness. The idea of humanity becomes superfluous. This kind of evil is more than power, selfishness, sadism, or egoism. It defies the very abilities of humans to categorize. It is this kind of evil that underlies the genocides that I explore in

15. Arendt, *The Origins of Totalitarianism.*
16. Formosa, "Is Radical Evil Banal? Is Banal Evil Radical?," 718.

chapter 3. For Arendt there was an inexplicability, perhaps even a demonic element to radical evil (although she never equated it with supernatural forces). Evil in this mode is the very manifestation of Paul's description of the intention of the powers in Ephesians: to destroy the good entirely; to destroy human being entirely.

The banality of evil

Arendt appeared to change her position on the inexplicability of evil as she watched the trial of Otto Adolph Eichmann in Jerusalem. Eichmann was a German-Austrian and one of the major organizers of the Holocaust. During World War II, Eichmann was tasked with facilitating and managing the logistics involved in the mass deportation of Jews to ghettos and extermination camps in Nazi-occupied Eastern Europe. After the war, he escaped to Argentina but was captured by the Israeli Mossad in May 1960. Eichmann was taken out of the country and put on trial in Jerusalem. He was later convicted, and in 1962 he was hanged. Arendt was sent by the *New Yorker* to report on the trial. Along with a series of articles she wrote a book that turned out to be highly controversial, titled: *Eichmann in Jerusalem: A Report on the Banality of Evil* (1964). The subtitle was the focal point for argument, controversy, anger, and misunderstanding.[17]

Prior to the trial, Arendt had expected Eichmann to be an amoral monster, a fitting player within the context of radical evil. However, as she sat in the courtroom and watched him over the course of the trial, she was surprised. He was not the amoral monster she assumed he would be. He was a bureaucrat interested in keeping the systems for which he was responsible running effectively. He was a man, a clown (as she described him), who seemed only able to speak in clichés. Clichés allow one to avoid the issues and pass the blame on to others, clichés like "I was only doing my job." Eichmann certainly facilitated deeds that were radically evil and, as Arendt would argue later, completely unforgiveable.

17. Ring, "Hannah Arendt and the Eichmann Controversy."

She suggested, however, that he did so *without evil intention.* He was an organizer. Meticulous in planning the times and places for trains to move and for people to be relocated, but (or so Arendt thought) he wasn't particularly rabid about the Nazi cause. He was more interested in doing his job well and progressing up the career ladder. She suggested that Eichmann's evil deeds were tied not to evil intent, but to *thoughtlessness*: an inability to think from the standpoint of other people. She didn't mean he was stupid. *He was simply lacking in empathy and judgment.* "Lacking this particular cognitive ability, he 'commit[ted] crimes under circumstances that made it well-nigh impossible for him to know or to feel that he [was] doing wrong.'"[18] Arendt described the kind of behavior manifested in Eichmann as *the banality of evil.* He was shallow, thoughtless, lacking in empathy, and above all almost completely lacking in judgment. This was not to belittle or minimize his crimes: it was simply to point out that in this case tremendous evil was in fact explainable and tied to a failure to recognize that banal actions can have deeply evil sequences.

Is there a contradiction?

This brief analysis of Arendt's thinking raises the important issue of whether there may be a clash here between radical evil and banal evil. However, any contradiction is more apparent than real. Not all perpetrators of evil are banal. Eichmann and Hitler (assuming the accuracy of Arendt's picture of Eichmann) are *two different types of perpetrator.* Likewise, thoughtlessness is not the cause of *all* forms of evil. Hitler and those who developed the idea of the so-called Final Solution were very thoughtful. Indeed, seven of the twelve men who came up with the Final Solution had doctorates. The problem was misplaced morality and distorted thinking.

The philosopher Paul Formosa argues that radical evil and the banality of evil are compatible concepts.[19] The banality of

18. White, "What Did Hannah Arendt Really Mean by the Banality of Evil?"

19. Formosa, "Is Radical Evil Banal? Is Banal Evil Radical?"

evil retains its very human character as something that people do, whether consciously or unintentionally. (This resonates with Paul's exposition of evil as something humans do.) Radical evil, on the other hand, retains a certain diabolical depth and demonic profundity.[20] Formosa uses the terms "diabolical" and "demonic" metaphorically. However, bearing in mind our previous discussion on Paul's understanding of sin as a power, we might read this more literally. When you get into a situation where you think no one is watching you, yielding to this diabolical power becomes very tempting. Evil is not only something people do but also a power that acts upon them.

To sum up: radical evil is a type of evil.[21] It can manifest itself as a large-scale political phenomenon, but it can also reveal itself in inhumane acts of human violence carried out by individuals or communities. Wherever and however radical evil manifests, some aspects of ideological commitment, dehumanization, violence, oppression, and, indeed, morality (i.e., a cause that makes you think that you are doing things for good reasons) will be tied into it. As far as conscious motives go, people feel they *really are* being moral. The power of radical evil, and certainly of sin as Paul understands it, is that it intrudes between good intentions and their lethal outcomes. In Paul's account, this is sin's "use" of the law to deceive and kill (Rom 7:11). The reason this is so important is that Paul doesn't locate evil or sin in bad motives: he maintains a surprisingly positive view of human beings (in line with this book's opening comments about creation being very good), and thus provides a way to account for the complexities of human actions and their outcomes. (We might think here of the way in which "aid" sometimes backfires and ends up hurting the very communities it is meant to help).

The banality of evil refers to *a type of perpetrator*,[22] one who thoughtlessly perpetrates evil under certain circumstances, someone who suffers from a remoteness from reality but does not

20. Formosa, "Is Radical Evil Banal? Is Banal Evil Radical?," 724.

21. Formosa, "Is Radical Evil Banal? Is Banal Evil Radical?," 726.

22. Formosa, "Is Radical Evil Banal? Is Banal Evil Radical?," 726.

necessarily possess an overtly pathological psychology. These two forms of evil are often deeply interconnected. We can illustrate this interconnectedness through an exploration of one particular form of evil: pornography.

Pornography is becoming increasingly mainstream and acceptable. Easy access via the internet has led to a phenomenal increase in usage, which has moved pornography from a relatively small and often stigmatised minority pursuit, to an acceptable way of finding gratification. Some might say: "What harm can there be in that? If people want to watch or to make pornography that is up to them. They are not doing any harm." Well, it may seem that way from a certain perspective, but watching pornography is an evil enterprise in ways that I suspect many people do not consider.

Pornography: Evil Is Just a Click Away

The rise of pornography use is quite startling. Some basic statistics will help make this point:

- Forty million adults regularly visit internet pornography sites.[23]
- Approximately eleven million teens access some form of pornography daily.
- Enough porn was watched in 2016 on one major website (Pornhub) that all the data would fill 194,000,000 USB sticks. If you put the USB sticks end to end, they'd wrap all the way around the moon.
- In 2017 alone, that same website (based in Canada) got 28.5 *billion* visits. That's almost one thousand visits per second, or 78.1 million per day—way more than the population of the entire United Kingdom. That number has since jumped massively to 33.5 billion site visits in 2018.
- In 2016, 91,980,225,000 videos were watched on Pornhub. In 2018, that number jumped to more than 109,012,068,000.

23. Logue. "Pornography Statistics."

That's over fourteen videos watched for every person on the entire planet.

- Over 5,824,699,200 hours of porn were watched on the site in just 2019. That's equal to almost 665 centuries of content consumed in one year. And all of that is on just one website!
- Every second:
  - £2,350/$3,193.30 is spent on pornography
  - 28,258 internet viewers look at pornography
  - 372 "adult" search terms are entered into search engines
- Every thirty-nine minutes a new pornographic video is made in the United States.[24]

One unrecognized "side effect" of the 2020 global pandemic was that because people were stuck at home and bored, traffic to one of the main porn sites increased by 22 percent in late March 2020.[25] Pornography is increasingly perceived as acceptable and mainstream, rather than stigmatized. What many people seem not to realize is how dangerous it is. Pornography is bad for your physical health, your mental health, and your spiritual health. This is bad enough, but it has even darker dimensions, as we shall see.

Porn and the brain

It is becoming more and more apparent that pornography is bad for the brain. Studies show that extensive use of pornography involves the same parts of the brain that are affected by other forms of addiction, such as drug and alcohol use:

> Through evolutionary design, the brain is wired to respond to sexual stimulation with surges of dopamine. This neurotransmitter, most often associated with reward anticipation, also acts to program memories and information into the brain. This adaption means that when the body

24. "How Many People Are on Porn Sites Right Now?"
25. "Pornography Is Booming during the COVID-19 Lockdowns."

> requires something, like food or sex, the brain remembers where to return to experience the same pleasure.[26]

The problem is that instead of turning to a romantic partner for love and connection, habituated porn users turn to their phones or computers and in a real sense use them to bond with multiple strangers. These frequent and powerful blasts of reward actually damage people's brains:

> Porn scenes, like addictive substances, are hyper-stimulating triggers that lead to unnaturally high levels of dopamine secretion. This can damage the dopamine reward system and leave it unresponsive to natural sources of pleasure.[27]

The consequences of this are that some youngsters are experiencing sexual dysfunction in their early teens. Other studies point out that these kinds of changes in our dopamine systems can lead to anxiety and depression.[28]

A problem of lust

Now that is telling enough. But there is more to the dangerous story of pornography. We might at first think that we are dealing here primarily with a problem of lust, and certainly many Christians think about pornography primarily through the frame of lust. Not so. In his recent book *Addicted to Lust: Pornography in the Lives of Conservative Protestants*, the social scientist Samuel L. Perry examined the use of pornography amongst conservative Christians in the United States. His research indicated that porn use by Christian men and women sits at around the average for the general population. However, among this population it has a more powerful negative effect in terms of mental health and the continuity and

26. Barr, "Watching Pornography Rewires the Brain to a More Juvenile State."

27. Barr, "Watching Pornography Rewires the Brain to a More Juvenile State."

28. Wilson, *Your Brain on Porn.*

integrity of personal identity. Living with the dissonance of using pornography while at the same time belonging to a faith that frames lust as a sin leads to anxiety and depression. Why? Because pornography is not just about what you watch: it's also about what it *means* to you and your community. That is the difference between Christians who watch pornography and non-Christians who engage in the same actions. There is an important paradox with conservative Protestants. They are a group who are vehemently against pornography on moral grounds. And yet, statistically they view pornography only a little less than the average person. This leads to conservative Christians who use porn having an increased likelihood of the symptoms of depression. Men feel that there is a deep sadness that they can't get away from, significant feelings of a loss of self-worth and guilt caused by having to lie and hide their actions. So, it seems that for Christians, watching pornography not only damages your brain, it also causes moral dissonance, anxiety, shame, and depression. This is a long way away from the life of love and flourishing towards which Scripture points us.

Pornography is a form of evil in which people are commodified for the purposes of encouraging and satisfying the lust of others. Pornography not only seeks to satisfy sexual desires, but it also actually creates new ones. As the brain gets used to certain images, the dopamine rush becomes lessened. We need stronger images in order to stimulate our dopamine production. This is why pornographers have to continually create images that are ever stronger and more graphic.

This sin of sexual lust is clearly more dangerous than some might presume. Not only does pornography distort our ability to see and respect the image of God in other people, it also has serious physical and psychological effects, particularly for Christians. We could just leave it there. Tragically, there is another dimension to pornography that is even darker: *the connection between pornography and sex trafficking.*

Pornography and sex trafficking

The organization Fight the New Drug notes that:

> The average porn consumer, likely exposed and hooked in before the age of 18, has no idea what exactly goes into the production of a single pornographic image or video. They might not even think about how or why a performer got to be on camera, or the situation that led them to their involvement with porn. If someone contributed even one, or a substantial amount, of the 42 billion visits to one of the world's most popular free porn sites in 2019, they probably don't understand the likelihood that they might be getting aroused by images of a performer who didn't appear on film under their own free will. *In other words, [they are] seeing a victim of human sex trafficking.*[29]

Exploiting human beings is big business. A study from the United Nations' International Labour Organization estimated 3.8 million adults and one million children were victims of forced sexual exploitation in 2016 around the world.[30] Although boys, men, trans, intersex, and nonbinary individuals can also be victims, 99 percent of the adults and children trafficked for sex are female.[31] The organization Human Rights First states that :

> An estimated 24.9 million victims are trapped in modern-day slavery. Of these, 16 million (64%) were exploited for labor, 4.8 million (19%) were sexually exploited, and 4.1 million (17%) were exploited in state-imposed forced labor.[32]

While only 19 percent of trafficking victims are trafficked for sex,

29. Fight the New Drug website, https://fightthenewdrug.org/ (accessed January 27, 2022, italics added).

30. Kelly, "13 Sex Trafficking Statistics That Explain the Enormity of the Global Sex Trade." *USA Today News* (accessed January 24, 2022).

31. Kelly, "13 Sex Trafficking Statistics."

32. "Human Trafficking by the Numbers."

> sexual exploitation earns 66% of the global profits from human trafficking. The average annual profit generated by each woman in forced sexual servitude ($100,000/£73,590) is estimated to be six times more than the average profits generated by each trafficking victim worldwide ($21,800/£16,043), according to the Organization for Security and Cooperation in Europe (OSCE) studies show that sexual exploitation can yield a return on investment ranging from 100% to 1000%.[33]

Human Rights First state that people who are trafficked earn $150,000,000,000 (£110,387,250,000) every year. And $99,000,000,000 (£72,896,175,000) of that relates to commercial sexual exploitation.[34] Not for themselves of course, but for big business and organized crime—*the purveyors of radical evil.*

In considering the relationship between pornography and sex trafficking, think for a moment what sex trafficking entails. It is not simply people being stolen from one country or location and forced to work in another, although clearly that is a significant aspect of it. The United Nations Office of Drugs and Crime defines human trafficking as:

> the recruitment, transportation, transfer, harbouring, or receipt of persons, by means of the threat or use of force or other forms of coercion, of abduction, of fraud, of deception, of abuse of power or of a position of vulnerability, or of the giving or receiving of payments or benefits to achieve the consent of a person having control of another person, for the purpose of exploitation. Exploitation shall include, at a minimum, the exploitation of the prostitution of others or other forms of sexual exploitation, forced labour or services, slavery or practices similar to slavery, servitude or removal of organs.[35]

Pornography relates to human trafficking in at least four ways:

33. "Human Trafficking by Numbers."

34. "Human Trafficking by Numbers."

35. United Nations Office of Drugs and Crime, "Trafficking in Persons: Universally Defined in the UN Trafficking in Persons Protocol."

First, nearly half of sex trafficking victims report that their traffickers filmed them in pornography.[36] Pornhub has recently had remove millions of videos following an investigation by the *New York Times*[37] and a separate investigation by Visa and Mastercard[38] following the discovery that videos of child abuse abduction and rape were being monetized on its website.[39] Take, for example, the case of a fifteen-year-old girl from Florida, who was missing for a year and was located after fifty-eight videos of her alleged sexual abuse and rape were found, monetized on Pornhub. The face of the child's alleged attacker was seen in the videos and matched by law enforcement to convenience store surveillance footage. He was eventually found and charged with a felony. "Pornhub had verified the child victim and accidentally admitted to complicity in her trafficking, but later deleted their admission."[40]

Second, traffickers use pornography to train sex trafficking victims to perform various sexual acts and situations. Thus, pornography feeds into the educational strategy of traffickers, with pornographers shaping and forming the tastes of their clients. Bearing in mind what we said previously about the brain and addiction, one can see that pornographers have to be constantly pushing the limits with the types of material they produce. This limit-pushing has dire consequences for the men, women, and children who are trapped in this modern-day slavery.

Third, 80 percent of survivors report that their customers showed them pornography to illustrate the kinds of sexual acts they wanted them to perform.[41]

36. "Pornhub under Investigation by Visa, Mastercard amid Abuse Allegations." Westbrook and Ven Dyke, "Why Do We Let Corporations Profit from Rape Videos?"

37. Kristof, "The Children of Pornhub."

38. "Pornhub Removes Millions of Videos after Investigation Finds Child Abuse Content."

39. Kristof, "The Children of Pornhub."

40. "One Million People Sign Petition to Shut Down Pornhub for Alleged Sex Trafficking Videos"; "Florida Man Arrested after Videos of Missing Teen Surface on Pornography Website."

41. "The Connection between Sex Trafficking and Pornography."

Fourth, sex trafficking, as illustrated in the above definition, relates to consent. If a person does not give consent, then they are being forced and coerced to give their labor. This is important, because some might argue that mainstream pornography is harmless because the people participating have consented. However, there are numerous stories of actors and actresses turning up for a shoot thinking they were going to do one thing and being coerced into doing something they did not want to do under threat of non-payment of wages, the end of their career, and so forth. So, consent even amongst professionals is not straightforward. The reality is that when people look at porn, they have no idea whether the people they are watching have consented or whether have been trafficked.

And here is the key point in relation to our discussion on the banality of evil: every click has advertising connected with it, and so any viewing of pornography is monetized. *Every click of the mouse funds the powers of darkness.* It may seem banal and harmless to sit in our homes clicking away, but when we realize the consequences, we can see that the apparent banality of the act of clicking a mouse significantly affects our mental health, changes the structure of our brains, and forces us to desire and indeed to crave things that are clearly not of God, and indeed leads us to believe that they are normal. It also feeds directly into the propagation of radical evil and the deconstruction and abuse of other human beings. *Radical evil is becoming mainstreamed.*

Of course, Christians are not silent on the issue of pornography. However, it is an issue we often primarily frame in terms of lust, morality, and the need to cease. It does of course relate to all of these things, and not watching it is definitely the cure. However, there is a much deeper and darker dimension that we miss at our peril. I suggest that we all warn our youngsters and perhaps take note ourselves of the apparent banality of mouse clicks and the dangers of the thoughtless, unintentional participation in evil that comes from not thinking through the effects of our individual, apparently small actions.

Gathering the Threads

The evils of poor judgment

If, with this in mind, we now return to Eastman's analysis of Paul's thinking on evil and sin and Arendt's observation on Eichmann and the banality of evil, we can begin to see how easy it is to be come implicit in the perpetration of evil without noticing it. The banality of evil is well illustrated in Paul's observation that you do not have to intend to be evil to be complicit with evil, something that has become clear in our brief exploration into the evil of pornography. As Eastman puts it:

> People consciously lie, and people also unconsciously act out the implications of living in a lie; this too for Paul is evil. Thus the common excuses, such as "I didn't mean to do it"; or "well, that's what I said but I didn't mean it," or, "I didn't know what I was doing," are simply irrelevant to questions of human culpability and divine judgment. Intentions are slippery if not impossible to pin down.[42]

At a minimum, Eichmann's cognition and vision had become distorted as he thoughtlessly gave himself over to the demonically warped description of the world that emerged from engagement with Nazi ideology. His failure to acknowledge *God*, name God *as God*, and accept that God cannot be reduced to the self, had disastrous consequences. The tight connection between distorted cognition, false speech, and evil acts led to a situation in which signing forms and shuffling pieces of paper resulted in the death of millions of people. We discover the same dynamic in the use of our computer mouse clicks whereby the act of simply "clicking around" actually perpetrates great evil and the destruction of the wellbeing of human beings, including ourselves. *To participate in evil you simply need to stop thinking.*

42. Eastman, "Empire of Illusion," 11.

Evil: explained, inexplicable, and unexplainable

Arendt's idea of the banality of evil and Eastman's emphasis on evil as distorted cognition remind us that evil can be understood in terms of where we place our allegiances and our implicit or explicit engagement in thoughtless actions. They remind us that evil actions are not necessarily intentional. One cannot accidentally commit genocide, but one can unintentionally contribute to its occurrence. As the philosopher Susan Nieman chillingly observes:

> The Holocaust was carried out by millions of people with trivially bad intentions like those of Eichmann, who did not actively will the production of corpses, but was willing to walk over them, literally, if it advanced his career; the lukewarm well-meaning bystanders who wrung their hands and retreated to inner emigration as the catastrophe around them grew; and people whose intentions were often exemplary, but whose mistakes of judgment led them to actions that produced the opposite of what they intended. There are any number of shapes in between, but these kinds of examples should suffice to show that where it really matters, intention may drop out entirely.[43]

Before we pass judgment, we might want to pause for a moment and consider what, for example, it means that the designer training shoes or the nice cheap shirt or jacket that you or I might decide to purchase on the high street, online, or at the mall are made by children who live in deep poverty and who are paid next to nothing for producing them. A swipe of a credit card feeds the market within which the evil of child poverty flourishes. And that is before we consider the ways in which our phones and tablets are produced. *The world (and ultimately God), will judge us by our actions, not by our intentions.*

43. Neiman, "Banality Reconsidered," 310.

Sin as a power: the externality of evil

Eastman notes an important shift in Romans. Following Paul's description of evil in chapters 1 to 3, evil drops out of his writing until we get to chapter 7, where it returns, this time tied in with sin and (once again) deception. However, there is an important shift in how he now understands sin and evil. Evil is no longer simply something that people do. Now, in Romans 7:19–21, evil is tied in with sin and what sin *does*, "counter to the wishes of the Self. Sin now performs the actions previously ascribed solely to human beings."[44] Evil has become extended and externalized. From that point on, Paul perceives sin as an active force that we must vigorously challenge and avoid. Sin is not only the opposite of loving service to God and others: now it is seen as a force that *actively* attempts to move people away from the love of God. It is this kind of sin that lurks behind radical evil.

We are of course not left without hope. The resolution of the tensions and paradoxes in Paul's account of sin and evil is to be found in the life, death, and resurrection of Jesus. Romans ends with a striking statement about God's victory over sin: "I want you to be wise about what is good, and innocent about what is evil. The God of peace will soon crush Satan under your feet." (16:19b–20a). Wisdom enables us not to yield to temptation. God delivers us from the power of evil. We will return to this point in more detail in chapter 4.

Conclusion: Resisting Evil

We have seen in this chapter that there are in Romans two different narratives about the relationship of human beings with sin and evil.

> In the first, human beings are culpable "sinners" in need of forgiveness, and redemption consists of deliverance from the justly deserved wrath of God, which falls on Christ rather than on us. Here human beings have, in

44. Eastman, "Empire of Illusion," 7.

> principle, the cognitive capacity to change and not to yield to temptation. They do this in conjunction with the Spirit, but there is meaningful bodily participation in our resistance. Our failures here are covered by the blood of Jesus. In the second narrative of sin and evil, human beings are enslaved and deceived by sin with sin perceived as a hostile power that co-opts even the best human endeavours. Redemption here consists of God's active deliverance from that enslaving power through union with Christ.[45]

To sum up:

1. *Evil is something that people do.* It is a choice rather than an inevitability. However, it is possible to do evil without intending to choose to do evil. Good judgment, discernment, critical thinking, and thoughtfulness are therefore primary ways of resisting the banality of evil.
2. *Sin is a power that destroys human goals, callings, and flourishing. Where sin is, evil will be there too.* Sin is a power that actively seeks to prevent humans from attaining their true heart's desire: to love God and others. As such, sin and evil require spiritual understanding and intervention as well as political, social, and psychological responses. Resisting evil requires embodied actions and spiritual warfare.
3. *Encountering sin is inevitable, but evil is not irresistible.* Doing evil is a temptation, a lure intended to distract us from doing what is right and good. But we can resist it by putting on the armor of faith. Ultimately, evil has been and will be defeated through the blood of Jesus.

In this chapter, we have begun to discern what evil is and what it does. In the next chapter we begin uncovering evil in everyday situations.

45. Eastman, "Empire of Illusion," 17.

2

The Banality of Evil

The COVID-19 Pandemic

In the previous chapter I developed an understanding of evil by exploring what it looks like, what it does, and how it is possible to become embroiled in it even if one does not intend to do so. Actions do not have to be intentional to be evil. I ended the chapter by highlighting the need to be thoughtful, discerning, and aware of the evil that is all around and within us, much of which we may not even notice. Now I turn to exploring what the outworking of *thoughtfulness*, *discernment*, and the *recognition* of evil looks like.

Living in a Time of Pandemic

As I write this chapter, we are going through a global pandemic caused by the coronavirus or COVID-19. Its impact on the world has been devastating. Global lockdowns, death on a large scale, social distancing, a cessation of public worship, and the concurrent damage done to the world economy have led to fear, anxiety, and deep uncertainty about the future. The sense of disorientation, disconnection, anxiety, and uncertainty is pervasive.

Theologically many of us are confused about why God would allow such a thing to happen, and what the coming of the virus and its accompanying destruction might mean for our understanding of God's love, power, presence, and goodness. The temptation in such difficult times is to look to the enterprise of theodicy to help us understand what is going on. "How could a loving all powerful God allow a pandemic?" is an understandable question. As modern people we have great difficulty in living with unanswered questions. We tend to turn mysteries into puzzles and try to solve them. That being so, the apparently "obvious" theological route to take in this time of pandemic is to fit it into the standard question of theodicy: *why has God allowed the pandemic to happen?* Here we simply assume that the pandemic is another example of the classical problem of evil with the solution being the fall, sin, human wickedness, God's judgment, and so forth. However, if we allow this kind of, in my view, unanswerable theological question to become the center of our attention, we risk being distracted from some of the less obvious evils that accompany the emergence of things like the pandemic. While we are wrestling with big, undoubtedly important, but ultimately unsolvable questions, evil can easily slip in through another door in a quite different guise. This chapter focuses on two different but connected questions:

- *What kind of evil emerged from within the pandemic?*
- *What did it do us?*

Recall that in the previous chapter I established that if we are to resist evil, we first need to see it, to recognize it. Thinking through these two questions on the nature of this evil and its effects on us provide a starting point for learning how to discern evil in everyday places.

The new norm?

I have been thinking quite a lot about the so-called "new norm" that people think will emerge when, or perhaps if, we finally get to grips with COVID-19. Perhaps readers of this book will already be living out this new norm. Or perhaps we will simply have gone back to the old norm, as if nothing enduring really happened. Many of us want to get back to the way things were. But I wonder, is the old norm really something to which we should aspire? We may be longing for "the good ol' days," but *were they actually all that good?* Maybe they were for some of us, but not for many and perhaps most of the human race.

Early on in the pandemic the Australian journalist John Pilger reminded us of what the "old norm" was *really* like:

> A pandemic has been declared, but not for the 24,600 who die every day from unnecessary starvation, and not for 3,000 children who die every day from preventable malaria, and not for the 10,000 people who die every day because they are denied publicly-funded healthcare, and not for the hundreds of Venezuelans and Iranians who die every day because America's blockade denies them life-saving medicines, and not for the hundreds of mostly children bombed or starved to death every day in Yemen, in a war supplied and kept going, profitably, by America and Britain. Before you panic, consider them.[1]

If Pilger is correct, one has to ask why it is that, first, many of us don't seem to know such dire statistics, and second, how those of us who do know such things manage to sleep at night. Paul's vision of evil as emerging from distorted thinking, occluded vision, and a handing over of ourselves to ways of seeing, thinking, and acting that privilege self over God may be closer to our reality than we like to admit. It could be that the "old norm" was in fact underpinned by an illusion behind which evil lurked in all of its poisonous radicality and banality. Perhaps the pandemic is causing that veil of illusion to slip, and what is revealed is not good.

In thinking through this suggestion, let me offer three movements that emerged from within the pandemic, but which will continue long after the virus has been controlled—assuming that does

1. Pilger, "Here Is What Legendary Journalist John Pilger Said about Coronavirus Outbreak."

in fact happen. These movements will help raise our consciousness about where our illusions lie and the places where evil has for a long time been present, albeit hidden from many of us. Mapping out these three movements will also point towards ways in which we can try to avoid simply reincorporating the same old evils within the "new norm" as it emerges. If you are reading this from within the "new norm," you can perhaps assess whether the illusions uncovered by the pandemic were taken seriously, or whether they're still being lived out. The movements are as follows:

1. *From passion to resurrection*
2. *From scarcity to abundance*
3. *From social distancing to loving trust*

Developing a Post-Pandemic Imagination

Movement 1: from passion to resurrection

What might it mean to develop a post-pandemic imagination? Imagination is of course vital to survive and make sense of the world. It would be very difficult to cross the road safely if we didn't have the kind of imagination that allows us to know that a road is full of cars, that these cars will all be traveling in particular directions on particular sides of the road, and that if they hit us we will be damaged or perhaps even killed. A failure of imagination even in such a basic thing as crossing the road can be deadly.

Our imagination comprises the values, expectations, images, methods, assumptions, and plausibility structures (i.e., what is plausible or implausible for us to believe) that allow us to understand and move through the world. Such things as family, culture, politics, economics, and religion shape our imaginations, for they all contain imagination-bearing stories that tell us about what the world is, how we should behave in certain circumstances, what we should and should not believe, and how we should or should not think and act. When in Romans 12 Paul talks about a renewed mind, in a sense he is talking about the ways in which knowledge of Jesus develops within us a restructured gospel imagination. As Christians engage with the gospel story and move through the process of sanctification in the power of the Spirit, so our minds and imaginations are transformed in ways that help us to recognize God and ourselves in such a way that we can learn to perceive and avoid evil and resist the power of sin. The more fully our minds are transformed, and our cognitive and relational misalignments are healed, the more effectively we see sin and evil.

A new situation, like the pandemic, is an opportunity for us to use the Scriptures, theology, and church practice to develop a faithful post-pandemic imagination. Such an imagination provides us with a way of prophetically re-imagining the world in the light of what we have learned about ourselves, others, the world, and God during the pandemic. In so doing we begin to see through some dangerous illusions.

The new norm, however, is not the old norm with a different hat on! I have already suggested that our old norm may have contained dangerous illusions. Shaping the new norm into the image of the old norm is therefore precisely what we must *not* do. Take as an example the passion of Jesus, beginning with Jesus's triumphal entry into Jerusalem (John 12:13). As Jesus entered the city, people were really excited! It was a time of great expectation. "The Messiah has come!" Then came the passion and the chaos of the cross. Everything seemed to be falling apart. All of the people's hopes, dreams, and expectations that were embodied in Jesus-the-Messiah seemed to come crashing down. For a while it felt as if there was nothing left but grief, sadness, lostness, pain, suffering, disappointment, and fear. Inevitably people feel deeply vulnerable when their hopes and certainties are crushed and their control over the world is stripped from them. No wonder Jesus's disciples were terrified, panicked, and hid.

But then came the resurrection. Jesus overcame death and in so doing offers us a new life: *the ultimate new norm!* Yet this new norm is not a return to the fanatical victorious hopes of Palm Sunday fervor. The crucifixion showed us the reality of pain and suffering and the lengths to which God will go to help us to find and to share in God's love. The nails piercing Jesus's hands shattered any utopian fantasies about the coming norm. The new norm heralded by the resurrection was very different from the old norm, both in quality and in kind. It was a call to go into the world proclaiming the gospel and the love of God in the midst of pain, suffering, and lostness, to battle evil and instead bring justice and healing. The new norm that Jesus's resurrection ushered in was a revelation: the power and might of God to overcome the evil, sin, and brokenness of human beings is revealed in vulnerability and suffering love, not in armies and oppression. The new norm enabled people to recognize their interconnection. It emphasized their life as one community, as Jesus's body, blessed and freed to live under the wing of God, who *is* love. The new norm called and still calls Christians to care for the sick, the weak, and the broken; to live life with and for others in a spirit of wisdom, gentleness, peace, love, and joy. It calls us not to a life of happiness and individual pleasure, but to a way of living in which it is normal to give up our lives for our friends (John 5:13). The new norm of resurrection life is not simply about solving the old problems and fulfilling human dreams, desires, and expectations coming true. No. It's about overcoming the old gods of greed, individualism, and false idols and living a life of love, compassion, and consideration for our neighbors, a life with God in the power of God's Spirit.

Do you see? There is both continuity and radical discontinuity between the Palm Sunday dream that emerged from human misunderstanding, and the resurrection life of divine grace. The latter wasn't quite as we had expected. As the new norm emerges, perhaps our experiences of the pandemic will reorient us; will help us stop falling in love with ourselves and our own needs and learn to see the world and others' needs more clearly. Perhaps it'll help us to live into the love of God and one another more fully. Our old norm included dangerous illusions. The new norm has to be built on stronger foundations.

"But what has this got to do with evil?" you may ask. Our second movement will help answer that question.

Movement 2: from scarcity to abundance: how the pandemic has challenged our assumptions that we truly do love our neighbors

Central to the gospel is the radical suggestion that we should *love our neighbors*. In Mark 12:30–31 Jesus tells us that the sum of the law and the prophets is to "'Love the Lord your God with all your heart and with all your soul and with all your mind and with all your strength.' The second [commandment] is this: 'Love your neighbor as yourself.' There is no commandment greater than these." These three dimensions of love are inextricably intertwined. As we come to know and to love God, we recognize that we are loved and valued and that we are worth loving. When being so loved sinks in, we begin to appreciate that our neighbor is also loved and worthy of love. These three dimensions of love form the heart of the gospel and shape and form the origins and nature of discipleship.

To me, one of the pandemic's saddest revelations is that love of neighbor may not be central to the way our society operates—and indeed may not be central to the way in which we *Christians* operate.

i. Anxiety, fear and scarcity: why the pandemic unleashed a frenzy of toilet-paper buying

Do you remember the controversy early on in the pandemic around hoarding toilet paper? As soon as the possibility of shortages was mentioned, people stripped the shops of toilet paper! They didn't seem to know why they needed to hoard toilet paper, but they definitely knew that it was important! Soon many more supermarket shelves were emptied as people began to hoard not just toilet paper but *everything*! Apparently, it didn't matter that there was enough food in the UK to feed everyone three times over. Evidently, it also didn't matter that by hoarding food (and toilet paper) people were jeopardizing the wellbeing of the most vulnerable people within our society—those without the financial capacity to stock up. In some ways it was funny. Why you need toilet paper to deal with an airborne virus is not clear. In other ways it most certainly was not funny. So, what was going on?

As the coronavirus began to spread across the western hemisphere, from February to March 2020, sales of toilet paper skyrocketed by up to 700 percent. This prompted psychologists to look at the reasons for such an odd phenomenon. Theo Toppe and his colleagues at the Max Planck Institute for Evolutionary Anthropology in Leipzig, Germany, surveyed 996 people in twenty-two countries across North America and Europe about how they purchased and stored toilet paper. Participants also ranked the threat of COVID-19 on a ten-point scale and took a test that rated them on several core personality traits.[2] These researchers found that

> People who felt threatened by COVID were more likely to hoard and people who tend to be more conscientious, that is those who are future-oriented and orderly, also tend to stockpile." . . . It's likely that anxious individuals were hoarding because it gave them a sense of control when so much was out of control. . . . The anxious among us might also have been more likely to wear masks and to stay a good distance from others when outside—that is, if they went outside their homes at all. . . . While the hoarding behavior may seem especially selfish, you have to remember that anxiety can be a powerful force . . . If you're super anxious, your brain can be hijacked by that fear, so you don't think about the societal impact [of actions like hoarding].[3]

The fear of the virus evoked anxiety, which in turn seemed to overpower any desire to love one's neighbor. When the chips are down, we are happy to love our neighbors, but *only* for as long as we are secure in the knowledge that our own needs are being met.

2. "Why the Pandemic Unleashed a Frenzy of Toilet Paper Buying."

3. Garbe, Rau, Toppe, "Influence of Perceived Threat of Covid-19 and HEXACO Personality Traits on Toilet Paper Stockpiling."

ii. Vaccine hoarding

Whilst there may have been a comical element to the hoarding of toilet paper, there was little humour to be found when we realised that exactly the same phenomenon was occurring in relation to the dispersal of vaccines across the world. In its annual report, Amnesty International noted that:

> Richer countries are failing a "rudimentary" test of global solidarity by hoarding Covid vaccines. . . . [Amnesty International] accused China and others of exploiting the pandemic to undermine human rights. . . . The health crisis had exposed "broken" policies and that cooperation was the only way forward. . . . "The pandemic has cast a harsh light on the world's inability to cooperate effectively and equitably," said Agnes Callamard, who was appointed Amnesty's secretary general last month. . . . "The richest countries have effected a near-monopoly of the world's supply of vaccines, leaving countries with the fewest resources to face the worst health and human rights outcomes.[4]

Instead of loving our neighbors, we are actually killing our neighbors through our selfishness, short-term thinking, and lack of awareness.

iii. Love ~~your neighbor as~~ YOURSELF

At one point the narrative began to change. Once we (the rich western world) began to realize the danger of mutations coming into our country from other infected areas, it became apparent that if everyone wasn't vaccinated then everyone remained in danger. So, the story changed to one of *self-interest*. We realized that if we didn't share first our knowledge about vaccines in development, and then the vaccines themselves, our tight-fistedness would work against *us*. We rich countries began to consider sharing our vaccines with

4. "'Amnesty International Condemns Rich Countries for Hoarding Covid-19 Vaccines."

poor countries *not because of love of neighbor, but because of love of self!* We turned Jesus's command to love God and neighbor upside down, and clearer thinkers revealed our apparent altruism as self-love: love of self without love of God and neighbor.

Our fear of the virus revealed something rather dark about our societies. And Christians were not immune to such tensions. A good Christian friend said to me at one point: "John, I was quite shocked with myself. I realized that I was thinking, 'If there is not enough food to go round, I will do *everything* I can to make sure my kids get it!' That's not me . . . ." But perhaps such thinking and actions *are* actually "more her" and "more us" than she and we might want to imagine. Christians are, after all, caught up in the same sin systems as anyone else. As Hebrew Bible scholar Walter Brueggemann puts it:

> We must confess that the central problem of our lives is that we are torn apart by the conflict between our attraction to the good news of God's abundance and the power of our belief in scarcity—a belief that makes us greedy, mean, and unneighborly. We spend our lives trying to sort out that ambiguity.[5]

As I write, we are once again in lockdown, and my local supermarket is, once again, rationing toilet paper and some foodstuffs. As the pandemic worsens and our anxiety grows, so our scarcity mentality increases in uncomfortable rhythm with the movement of the virus.

iv. Scarcity mentality

The virus exposed something within our culture that is deeply troubling. That something is our reactions that betray our *scarcity mentality*. Brueggemann notes that we

> hardly notice our own prosperity or the poverty of so many others. The great contradiction is that we have more and more money and less and less generosity—less

5. Brueggemann, "The Liturgy of Abundance, The Myth of Scarcity."

> and less public money for the needy, less charity for the neighbor.[6]

In times of perceived shortage, our generosity becomes the first casualty. In situations where scarcity is perceived, whether rightly or wrongly, we learn a lot about our priorities and we discover a lot about ourselves.

Brueggemann's point is that for many of us in the West, scarcity and the perception of possible scarcity elicit anxiety, greed, and the desire to horde. This is so even if such scarcity is illusory. He notes that what is true of the contemporary western world (and of course it is primarily a problem for rich people because if you have nothing, or very limited resources, you can't horde) has an analogue in the ancient people of Israel. They developed a remarkably similar scarcity mentality. They constantly lived in fear that they wouldn't have enough. Even when they did have enough, they lived in fear of losing it. What's so strange about this fear is that *they worship a God who promises abundance and yet they live in fear of scarcity.* What is true for the people of Israel is also true for many westerners today. Brueggemann continues:

> Today, the fundamental human condition continues to be anxiety, fueled by a market ideology that keeps pounding on us to take more, to not think about our neighbor, to be fearful, shortsighted, grudging. Over and over, we're told to be sure we have the resources to continue our affluent lifestyles, especially with the approach of our "golden years" (which are "golden" in more ways than one). That same market ideology powers the multinational corporations, as they roam the world, seeking the best deal, the greatest return, the cheapest labor and materials. Whether it's global policies or local poverty-wage jobs, those who fear scarcity refuse to acknowledge any abundance that extends beyond their own coffers.[7]

The more we have, the more anxious we become. The more we gain, the more we fear losing it. It's almost as if money and goods

6. Brueggemann, "The Liturgy of Abundance, The Myth of Scarcity."

7. Brueggemann, "The Liturgy of Abundance, The Myth of Scarcity."

function as a drug that draw us towards them, no matter the cost to others.

Biblically, the rich rely on an imagination that is fuelled by the fear of scarcity. The poor rely on an imagination that is dependent on abundance.[8] How can this be?

> The issue involves whether there is enough to go around—enough food, water, shelter, space. An ideology of scarcity says no, there's not enough, so hold onto what you have. In fact, don't just hold onto it, hoard it. Put aside more than you need, so that if you do need it, it will be there, even if others must do without. An affirmation of abundance says just the opposite: Appearances notwithstanding, there is enough to go around, so long as each of us takes only what we need. In fact, if we are willing to have but not hoard, there will even be more than enough left over. The Bible is about abundance. From the first chapters of Genesis, God not only initiates abundance—calling forth plants and fish and birds and animals—but promises continued abundance by commanding them to "increase and multiply" (1:22). God's generosity and fidelity reach their climax on the sixth day, when God proclaims a sufficiency for "everything that has the breath of life" and declares all this "very good" (1:30–31).[9]

If we were willing to have and not hoard, to share and not withhold, to be generous and not be selfish, things would be very different. The problem is *our lack of generosity.*

v. Pharaoh's anxiety

Brueggemann notes that the Bible starts out with a liturgy of abundance. Genesis is a song of praise about God's generosity. However, when we come to the exodus story, we find the introduction of another dynamic: Pharaoh enslaves the people of Israel and introduces the principle of scarcity into the world economy. For the

8. Brueggemann, "The Liturgy of Abundance, The Myth of Scarcity."
9. Brueggemann, "The Liturgy of Abundance, The Myth of Scarcity."

first time in the Bible, someone says, "There's not enough. Let's get everything."[10] Pharaoh fears that there is not enough to go around, so he has to have *all of it*! In the book of Exodus, we therefore find a battle between scarcity and generosity. That Exodus tension between generosity and the desire to hoard continues today:

> Possessing land, property, and wealth makes people covetous, the Bible warns. . . . We [America] who are now the richest nation are today's main coveters. We never feel that we have enough; we have to have more and more, and this insatiable desire destroys us. Whether we are liberal or conservative Christians, we must confess that the central problem of our lives is that we are torn apart by the conflict between our attraction to the good news of God's abundance and the power of our belief in scarcity—a belief that makes us greedy, mean, and unneighborly. We spend our lives trying to sort out that ambiguity.[11]

This is a quite remarkable situation! The people whom God has called to be generous refuse to be so primarily because the competitive market economy that underpins our culture suggests that such generosity is foolishness and that, even though we have much, we had better make sure that we have enough for every emergency, and for a holiday, a car, a night at the cinema . . . . And yet in 2 Corinthians 9:13 we find Paul saying this: "As a result of your ministry, they will give glory to God. For your *generosity* to them and to all believers will prove that you are obedient to the good news of Christ." Generosity is a mark of obedience and a revelation of the true nature of God. To live ungenerously is to place self before God and to mistake the things of God for the desires of human beings.

It is not difficult to see the *power* of sin at work here. The problem is not simply that you or I may not be generous. Lack of generosity is not simply a personal flaw. Much more substantially, *it is a cultural norm that manifests itself in individuals*. The

10. Brueggemann, "The Liturgy of Abundance, The Myth of Scarcity."

11. Brueggemann, "The Liturgy of Abundance, The Myth of Scarcity."

problem is that we have set up our entire system to encourage self-interest and personal success, usually for the strong and the powerful. We have based the system on the assumption that we need more "stuff" to be happy and that if we have more "stuff" we can find security, prosperity, and safety, and in so doing fend off our fear and anxiety. Our capitalist system does not teach us to love our neighbor as a *first principle*. We love ourselves first and *if* we are prosperous *then*, perhaps, we can—if we choose to—share some of that wealth with others. The system in fact *requires* that we remain fearful, short-sighted, and grudging, and that we do everything we can to retain our affluent norm. Of course, this affluent norm is not available to everyone, but most of us still aspire to it as if that were the norm. The problem is that many of us are so used to this being normal that we don't notice how abnormal and illusory it actually is. We may laugh and pass judgment on the toilet paper hoarders, but their behavior is symptomatic of something much deeper, much more problematic, and much more corporate than we might at first assume.

If God's desire is for us to flourish, and if flourishing relates to maximizing our love for God, neighbor, and self, a lack of generosity is clearly a mode of individual and corporate evil that leads to a lack of flourishing in all people, but particularly the weakest and most vulnerable people within our societies. If Susan Eastman is correct in suggesting that for Paul the primary problem for human beings lies in their "failure to acknowledge God, name God as God, and accept that God cannot be reduced to the self,"[12] then to acquire money and goods for their own sake, to ignore the plight of the poor, to refuse to be charitable to our neighbor is far from God's desire. Surely acquisitive hearts and ungenerous relationships are the manifestation of individuals and a society that stand against God? The virus has revealed something about us as individuals and as a society that is not only uncomfortable, but clearly *evil*. It may be hidden well. It may simply be "the way that we think things are." But if we prod things a little, we begin to see that thinking in such a way is dangerous

12. Eastman, "Empire of Illusion," 5.

and illusory. Countering this kind of evil—an evil that feels normal and banal—requires that we develop a generous imagination and a plentiful spirit that drives us to act generously in a world that struggles to understand the centrality of generosity. When we are generous with our goods, our money, our time, our words, ourselves, our prayers, then we crush evil. When we refuse to be generous, evil flourishes. This is important to note in general terms, but it will become particularly important as the financial and relational implications of the pandemic emerge over the coming months and years. *Be alert! Be generous! Resist evil!*

Movement 3: from social distancing to loving trust: stay at home, protect the NHS, save lives, prepare for evil . . .

When the pandemic first hit, the UK government came up with the slogan: *Stay at home. Protect the NHS. Save lives.* The NHS is the acronym for the British healthcare system: The National Health Service. The fear was that the NHS would be overwhelmed by ill people if measures were not taken to reduce infection rates. So, lockdown—forcing people to stay at home for an extended period of time—and social distancing became mandatory along with mask wearing, which came in a little later. As the pandemic developed, the government changed its slogan to: *Stay alert. Control the virus. Save lives.* Many of us struggled to work out what it meant to "stay alert" to a virus, but the government insisted that the British people would understand what they meant. (We didn't.) However, as will become clear as this chapter develops, the government may have been on to something, even if not in the way they intended.

The *third movement* I want us to consider is the movement from social distancing to loving trust. As we have seen, love is the heart of the gospel. Rather than being merely an idea or a concept, love is an embodied practice the contours of which we learn as we engage with other people, communities, culture, and the world. Love is an act of imagination in which we use our bodies, our minds, and our hearts to engage with one another in quite particular ways. The bodily movements of love are very subtle but remarkably powerful. Love is communicated not just through our words, but also in and through the subtle movements of our bodies, the inflections of our language, the movements of our eyes, as we engage with one another as fully embodied human beings.

Likewise, trust and being together emerge over time as we learn how to be with one another safely. Trust requires non-anxious presence. Trust is communicated through relationships, experience, touch, distance, and the long-term outcomes of being together. Gestures of trust such as shaking hands are an embodied manifestation of trust that serves a significant social function in terms of bonding and creating trusting relationships in the long and the short term. The question is: what are the long-term implications of never again being (or feeling) able safely to shake hands with one another? Greeting parishioners at the church door with a fist or elbow bump has a very different feel to locking together palms and fingers in a trusting, deeply personal embrace. Praying together at a safe distance has a quite different feel to huddling together, clasping our Bibles with our heads bowed in the intimacy of shared devotion. It makes a difference if I feel that giving you a Bible might cause you deadly harm. There are very real dangers and very real opportunities for evil to thrive.

i. Social distancing v. physical distancing

One way of highlighting the dangers of the way that things are changing is to think through the implications of the emphasis on social distancing. Distancing in order not to infect others is obviously necessary in terms of public health during a pandemic. However, we really don't know the long-term psychological and social consequences of social distancing. What will happen if we continue to assume implicitly or explicitly that everyone, including our family and friends, are potential threats to our well-being? Jesus commands us to love our enemies (Matt 5:44). But that becomes complicated when our "enemies" are potentially *everyone*. Distancing in a time of pandemic is clearly necessary to protect our neighbor from harm. But *will we be able to stop doing it?* There is a danger that distance and distrust of the other becomes part of the new norm. The problem is that *social distancing has side effects.* Think about it this way: there is a difference between *social* distancing and *physical* distancing. Physical distancing is a public-health term that describes a behavior intended to stop us being infected by and passing on the virus. That is completely appropriate. To stop the spread, we must keep a distance from people for the sake of their health and our own. That this may include people we love is particularly painful, but it's necessary to be true to Jesus's command to love God, neighbor, and self.

However, *social* distancing is a relational term that refers to the nature of our social relationships. Early on in the pandemic government and health authorities encouraged us not to engage with close family and friends outside of our households or our pods. But most of us really do not want to get into the habit of social distancing, even if physical distancing may be an ongoing necessity.

During lockdown, I spoke to an elderly woman—I'll call her Amanda—about social distancing (she was in her doorway, and I was walking past doing my one hour of daily exercise). She just laughed! "I have been in social isolation for the past ten years! People have become experts at socially distancing themselves from me. But now with the coming of the virus, suddenly everyone wants to help me. It's odd really." I felt a bit bad as I was probably one of the "social distancers" to whom she was referring. She lives only a few hundred yards away from my house and it took a pandemic for me to notice her. The notion that she and many others amongst us are so vulnerable to being lonely, isolated, friendless, and not being noticed took me aback. Even more shocking to me was that Amanda had become used to being lonely. She was genuinely surprised when people started to pay attention to her.

Loneliness is one of the most painful experiences for human beings. We are made for community: "It is not good that humans should be alone" (Gen 2:18, author's adaptation). Our natural state is to be in relationship, *to belong.* We *belong* to God, we *belong* to creation, we *belong* to one another. In order to feel that we belong, people need to affirm us, to notice us, and to offer the gifts of time and friendship. To belong is to be loved. Amanda had had very little experience of receiving the fruits of the practices of belonging, but when things changed radically and suddenly with the pandemic, all at once people wanted to find out about her and help her. Potentially that's a beautiful thing—but only if it continues. How awful to find company during a crisis only for it to disappear when things get back to "normal." The revived sense of community and interdependency that has emerged during this time of COVID-19 is a gift that we must work not to lose as we move towards healthier times.

ii. Losing trust

Physical distancing is something we do for health reasons. Social distancing can easily become a mindset or a worldview, which can be quite unsafe. Viewing others as potential dangers to ourselves or our families erodes *trust*. Relationships are held together by a myriad of social cues, such as eye contact, bodily movements, shared understandings about boundaries, common assumptions, and, importantly, appropriate bodily contact. If I feel that I can't hug my mother for fear of infecting her or of being infected, that changes something very profound within our relationship. When loved ones and strangers become potential sources of danger, that inevitably affects our ability to trust. Trust is like a muscle. If we don't use it, it atrophies and dies. A world without trust is a very dangerous place to be. As *Guardian* columnist Rafael Behr puts it: "We must not underestimate the aggregate effect of curtailing millions upon millions of micro-niceties, even if we cannot predict what the impact will be. After the rules of lockdown are eased, the cordon sanitaire will remain in our minds."[13]

Physical distancing is necessary for our physical health. But in the long term, I believe that *social* distancing represents a threat to the future of trust:

13. Behr, "The Lockdown in Our Minds Will Be the Last Restriction to be Lifted."

> Some habits of trust might have to be relearned. It might require effort on a political and individual level to practice social un-distancing—to reach out of our digital boltholes. Repairing the damage done by this disease will be a project of cultural reconnection, not just economic redistribution. We will need new ways to feel joined for as long as we cannot take each other by the hand.[14]

Social distancing risks leading to a serious breakdown of trust at a personal and cultural level. However, there is another dimension to social distancing that affects trust, generosity, hospitality, and the formation of evil. This dimension is a little less obvious.

Mistrusting Strangers: The Behavioral Immune System

In Hebrews 13:2 the writer urges us: "Do not forget to show hospitality to strangers, for by so doing some people have shown hospitality to angels without knowing it." There is something profoundly important about offering hospitality towards those whom we do not know. It is as we offer such hospitality that we learn what it means to *feel* the love of God. The pandemic may be eroding such hospitality in fundamental ways. In the quotation above, Behr states that even after lockdown ends and things go back to "normal," "the *cordon sanitaire* will remain in our minds." This is an important observation. The cordon sanitaire is a guarded line preventing anyone from leaving an area infected by a disease and thus spreading it. So, the local lockdowns during the pandemic would be an example of the cordon sanitaire, as would quarantine restrictions. However, Behr's concern is not simply with physical boundaries, but also with *psychological* ones. There is some interesting psychological research that looks at the connection between health and physical difference. Take, for example, the issue of online dating. A recent article produced by the BBC showed that:

14. Behr, "The Lockdown in Our Minds Will Be the Last Restriction to be Lifted."

> In both online profiles and face-to-face meetings, Natsumi Sawada at McGill University in Canada has found that we form worse first impressions of other people if we feel vulnerable to infection. Further research has shown that conventionally less-attractive people are judged especially harshly—perhaps because we mistake their homely features for a sign of ill health.[15]

The less attractive you are (by conventional standards), the less people trust you. The reason seems to be that subconsciously people who have unconventional appearances can be linked to our innate fear of infections. The prettier or more handsome you are, the more people trust you. Why? Because you look healthy. Now, why might this be? At least a part of the reason lies in our evolutionary past. You can understand how we might have evolved to associate social distancing with suspicion of others. We obviously don't want to be allowing predators or sick people into our social space. So, we have developed an inbuilt wariness towards strangers, which makes social distancing from outsiders and strangers potentially beneficial. Of course, it depends on whom you define as "the stranger" and why.

The behavioral immune system

What is true for online dating seems also to be true for health, hygiene, disease, and sickness. The psychologist Mark Schaller has developed the idea of the *behavioral immune system*,[16] referring to a cluster of psychological mechanisms that allow organisms to detect the presence of harmful diseases, parasites, and/or disease-ridden substances. At its simplest level, the behavioral immune system prompts us to experience disgust and to recoil from a foul smell or to feel revulsion when seeing a pox (a virus such as chicken pox)

15. Robson, "The Threat of Contagion Can Twist Our Psychological Responses to Ordinary Interactions, Leading Us to Behave in Unexpected Ways."

16. Schaller, "The Behavioural Immune System and the Psychology of Human Sociality."

and the pustules that accompany it.[17] The benefits of this mechanism are obvious. Illness is an individual and a communal threat to survival and wellbeing. The problem with this mechanism or response is that it doesn't like to take chances, and therefore errs on the side of caution. This has significant consequences for individuals, communities, and for political systems. Healthy forms of social distancing can give way to unhealthy forms of social marginalization and unhealthy forms of political action.

Pathogens and parasites are too small for us to see unaided, so the behavioral immune system must make decisions about the nature of what we see and whether it is a threat. It must infer the presence of pathogens. The behavioral immune system can quite easily be hijacked into thinking that certain groups are unclean and appropriate objects of avoidance. So, for example, some of us may consider homeless people, people of another color or race, or people with facial disfigurements potentially pathogenic and best to avoid, even when in fact the threat of harm is unfounded. Writing in *Psychology Today*, Joshua Rottman points out that in his research,

> children and adults from the United States and India were less likely to trust information that was provided by people who were sick or unclean. Furthermore, our participants judged these sick or unclean people to be meaner, greedier, lazier, less smart, less brave, and less desirable to befriend. These biases against physically dirty and ill people emerged by the age of 5.[18]

There is also an uncomfortable connection between the stimulation of the behavioral immune system and the background to preparing the ground for historical atrocities. It is no coincidence that Nazi propaganda called Jews a "people of contagion" and Rwandan genocide participants called Tutsis "cockroaches." This kind of language talks directly to the behavioral immune system, often with horrendous consequences. Likewise, if we think about recent horrible manifestation of xenophobia against east Asian people, we

17. Rottman, "Is Covid-19 Inflaming Prejudice?"

18. Rottman, "Is Covid-19 Inflaming Prejudice?"

can see why the term "Chinese virus" specifically associates certain people as unclean, something that resonates powerfully with the behavioral immune system. We can easily see how such fear of infection could work itself out in other groups such as refugees, asylum seekers, and people of color.

Politics, health inequalities, and racism

All of this relates to the political realm in important ways. Take the issue of health inequality and racism. Here Rottman makes an interesting observation:

> All of this evidence suggests that heightened anxiety about the novel coronavirus may be contributing to heightened manifestations of bias. Especially given that people of color have been disproportionately struck by COVID-19, it seems possible that prejudice and discrimination have been compounded during recent weeks due in part to a chronic upregulation of behavioral immune systems. Clearly, there are many factors that have contributed to the unspeakably tragic killings of George Floyd, Breonna Taylor, and numerous others. Racial prejudices and police brutality have long predated the appearance of COVID-19, of course, but it's possible that the coronavirus has fueled them further.[19]

The point is not that the virus causes racism, but that it can feed into it if it is framed in particular ways. We need, for example, to be very careful when we discuss the fact that far more people of color are living and dying with the virus. If we develop a cultural imagination that implicitly or explicitly sees one group of people as more diseased than another, we can easily lay the foundations for dangerous responses and toxic politics that flourish on misinformed and frankly evil attitudes. The virus does not cause toxic politics, but once again, it contributes to a context that sows negative political seeds, which in turn end up in acts of evil and/or systems that support evil. The virus can thus be seen as having

19. Rottman, "Is Covid-19 Inflaming Prejudice?"

"side effects" that have significant and often unseen implications for both church and society.

Toxic politics

This suggestion of a connection between the pandemic and toxic politics takes us to one final dimension of social distancing, evil, and the behavioral immune system that we must consider. We have seen that at an individual level the behavioral immune system underpins certain feelings of disgust, recoil, and avoidance. But it also has an impact on people's moral and political views:

> Evolutionary biologists have observed a cross-cultural and historical correlation between the prevalence of infectious disease and authoritarian politics. The theory posits that "pathogen stress" leads to a more aggressive behavioural immune response, making societies less open, less tolerant and readier to sacrifice liberties for collective protection.[20]

In times of deep insecurity and fear, people tend to become more conservative and more willing to follow authority figures. This can lead to dangerous toxic forms of politics. It is not necessary to be an evolutionary biologist or a behavioral psychologist to realize that chronic anxiety and insecurity can provide an ideal context for noxious politics. If we look across Europe and increasingly within the United States, the rise of xenophobia, racism, white supremacism, nationalism, and far right politics has clearly increased since the insecurities that accompanied the financial crisis of 2007 to 2008. The coronavirus adds another layer to this anxiety and insecurity and contributes to an ever more fearful environment, not just within Europe, but across the globe. When people are afraid, they tend to vote in particular ways and defer to authorities in ways that they may not under other circumstances. This makes all of us vulnerable to the creation of political systems and innovations

20. Rottman, "Is Covid-19 Inflaming Prejudice?"

within systems that may well inhibit the kind of flourishing that God desires for God's creatures.

As I say, the virus does not *cause* toxic politics, but it clearly speaks into the formation of a context that is ripe for the sowing of negative and dangerous political seeds. This can only get worse as the financial dimensions of the coronavirus pandemic come to the fore over the next few months and years. It may be that evil is already lurking on our political horizons, somewhat banally for the moment, but not necessarily so for the future. This is why we need to think carefully about how it might be possible to move from social distancing to loving trust.

Conclusion: *Stay Alert, Control the Virus, Save Lives*

As I mentioned earlier, some of us were rather mystified by the UK government's change of slogan from "Stay at home, protect the NHS, save lives," to "Stay alert, control the virus, save lives." I asked: what exactly does it mean to stay alert to a virus? Well, maybe on reflection it wasn't such a bad idea. In light of the things that we have explored in this chapter, it may be that staying alert to the virus and its hidden spiritual, political, and social side effects is quite apposite. Even Peter said: "Be alert and of sober mind. Your enemy the devil prowls around like a roaring lion looking for someone to devour" (1 Pet 5:8). We need to be alert to the fact that social distancing has side effects and that these side effects can be deep conduits into hidden forms of evil, both banal and potentially radical. Paul was quite right to observe that evil is not always obvious. It is not necessarily intentional. But it is always deadly. How then do we find our way out of the empire of illusion and live lives of generosity, love, security, and trust that reveal the God who has overcome all evil?

Paul suggests that we renew our minds and develop a different kind of imagination (Rom 12:2). Amid current anxiety and the unusual cultural stimulation of the behavioral immune system, our task is to be like Jesus. Jesus responded to those living with culturally stigmatized illnesses such as leprosy not by recoiling or stigmatizing, but by deliberately moving towards them (Matt 8:3) and offering them hope, trust, and generous love. He pushed beyond "natural" responses, cultural barriers, and political assumptions towards the person behind the condition. We are not bound by our biological impulses. When we think about how best to love our neighbor during a pandemic, we need learn how to be with *and* to talk about one another in ways that bring healing and not fear. Presence matters. Words matter. Words create worlds.

In this chapter we have focused on the ways in which the virus has raised crucial issues in relation to how we deal with present and advancing evil, some of which is banal, some less so. We have concentrated on generosity, trust, security, hospitality, and the welcoming of strangers, and have seen how all these modes of resistance to evil are under attack with the coming of the pandemic. What we need to do now is move beyond the everyday forms of evil that surround us and begin to explore what evil looks like when it has no desire to hide. In the next chapter we therefore think about *radical evil.*

3

The Radicality of Evil

The Rwandan Genocide

My mother is 98 years old and lives on her own in a little town just outside of Aberdeen. She is amazing for her age. She has lived through a lot of things, both good and bad, but still lives a life filled with grace, humility, and faith. She is my spiritual hero. Most of the good things in me I have learned from her.

Yet she often complains about society and how it was never like this "in the old days." I know what she means. She lives in a beautiful rural part of Aberdeenshire in Scotland and her upbringing in the central belt of Scotland was much less complicated and, in many ways, better than it is for many of us today. But then I remind her of the wars that have gone on during her lifetime. If I am feeling really mean, I also remind her that the twentieth century has been the era of genocide, an era in which more human beings have been killed by other human beings than at any other period in history. In her lifetime there have been at least seven genocides and 11.5 million lives lost. Were these really better days? To my question she typically responds with a smile and says, "Just leave me with my illusion of goodness. I know how the world is, but if I thought about it too much, I'd just cry . . . ."

What is true for my mum is probably true for many of us. We hold on to the illusion of goodness, because to look beyond that would be to enter a vale of tears that might just swallow us up. But if we dare to peer beyond the illusion of goodness, what we see is not good. The recent past has been filled with unending wars, violence, and suffering. The statistics for genocide alone are stunning:

- Bosnia-Herzegovina (1992 to 1995)—200,000 deaths
- Rwanda (1994)—800,000 deaths
- Pol Pot's reign in Cambodia (1975 to 1979) —2,000,000 deaths
- Nazi Holocaust (1938 to 1945)—6,000,000 deaths
- Rape of Nanking (1937 to 1938)—300,000 deaths
- Stalin's Forced Famine (1932 to 1933)—7,000,000 deaths
- Armenians in Turkey (1915 to 1918)—1,500,000 deaths

This level of death and suffering is incomprehensible. Well, actually it's become entirely comprehensible, which is why it is so frightening. The tragedy of the post-Holocaust cry of "Never again!" is that it seems to have been replaced by a lament of "Again and again!" Human beings have an unfortunate propensity for wiping out other groups of human beings for political, religious, colonial, or economic gain. Evil may well manifest itself in the banality of our everyday actions, but there is another dimension to evil that is far from ordinary: *radical evil.*

In this chapter I will use the example of the Rwandan genocide of 1994, not only to show radical evil at work, but also to indicate how it may well be at work today within our own lives, our own communities, and our own countries. More than that, I will argue that Christians—you and I—are already implicated in it. It would be comforting to think that the people of Rwanda were somehow totally different from "us". However, as we will see, that is not the case. Given the right historical, political, economic, and theological circumstances it may well be that we are all capable of terrible things.

Rwanda might seem a long way away, both in terms of history and geography, but if we don't learn the lessons of history and recognize the problems of geographical distance then the danger of repeating mistakes is ever present. Ugandan Catholic priest and theologian Emmanuel Katongole points to the ways in which modern Western people have a tendency to avoid exploring difficult and complex issues by remaining silent. This silence manifests itself in at least two ways: *the silence of history* and *the silence of geography.*

Silence

The silence of history

The silence of history assumes that tragedies such as the genocide in Rwanda simply "happened." In terms of reporting the genocide in Rwanda, Katongole notes that historically there has been a tremendous silence in the various debates around the genocide. People seemed to assume that the 1994 genocide came out of nowhere.[1] Many of us today simply take that silence for granted, thus abrogating the possibility of historical responsibility for what went on and maintaining a thin and narrow historical perspective that places the blame for the genocide fully on the shoulders of the warring parties. We see the same kind of dynamic in the "war on drugs," the "war on terror," problems around poverty and race, and so forth, where we silence huge swaths of history to make way for a thin political narrative that attributes blame in ways that are simplistic, defensive, and usually destructive. However, Katongole points out that if we don't listen to history, we really can't hope to understand the present.

1. Katongole and Wilson-Hartgrove, *Mirror to the Church*, 77.

The silence of geography

The silence of history refuses to listen to the past. The silence of geography assumes that something like the Rwandan genocide was an isolated event that happened "over there." "It happened in a place completely unlike the ones "we" know.[2] My friend and New Testament scholar Beverly Gaventa wrote to me after I delivered the series lectures that lie behind this book. She was deeply concerned about some of the political changes emerging within American society and the deep fragmentation that had been revealed by the pandemic, combined with the violence against people of color that had been in the headlines at that time. She was concerned about these things. But she was also concerned about her reaction to my lectures:

> What disturbs me in my own response to your lecture is that I had such a hard time even thinking about pornography or about genocide elsewhere because of the domestic situation. I do, to be sure, try to keep up with international news. That's not the issue. The issue is that I discovered in myself a certain impatience with your focus. I hope you'll be aware that this is not at all a complaint about your lecture. Far from it! It's a reflection, or I think it may be, on the way in which evil consumes us so that we can barely see beyond our own horizon.[3]

This is an interesting reflection. The silence of geography does not necessarily emerge from an uncaring spirit. It can be a manifestation of anxiety and of an overwhelming fear of what is happening in one's own geographical location that prevents one from considering other geographical areas, even if one acknowledges their importance. Once again, we can see that the system of beliefs, experiences, and actions in which we are immersed can prevent us from seeing and responding to evil, or though seeing it being unable to respond. The problem of silence and inaction is

2. Katongole and Wilson-Hartgrove, *Mirror to the Church*, 77.

3. Beverly Gaventa. Personal correspondence. Used here with permission.

corporate and deeply tied in with Paul's ideas of sin as a power or a system beyond our control.

What happened in Rwanda is important not only because it is deeply painful and tragic, but also because, if we overcome our silence, it can reveal to us some vital issues that are crucial for recognizing and overcoming evil. As Katongole puts it:

> When we overcome these silences of history and of geography and look honestly at the story of genocide in Rwanda, we begin to realize that Rwanda is not as far away as we might imagine. In truth, the story of Rwanda reflects the same patterns of identity formation that are found in the West.[4]

If we are to understand some of the dynamics of the genocide, we need to say a little more about radical evil.

Radical Evil

In my earlier exploration of the thinking of Hannah Arendt, I touched on the idea of radical evil.[5] Arendt argued that this form of evil emerges via a three-step process:

Step one is *the killing of the juridical person*. Here, a person is stripped of any legal rights as a citizen of the country. They no longer count before the law. As Formosa puts it: "As far as the law is concerned such superfluous people simply do not exist. Concentration camps serve this end practically by creating an environment where any pretext to having rights is completely abolished."[6] It is therefore vital that people are not incarcerated in prison camps for any *legal* reason. Their imprisonment must make no sense. Imprisonment is completely arbitrary.

Step two involves *the killing of the moral person*. To be moral one needs to have the choice to do either good or evil. People living

4. Katongole and Wilson-Hartgrove, *Mirror to the Church*, 78.
5. Arendt, *The Human Condition*.
6. Formosa, "Is Radical Evil Banal?," 718.

within a totalitarian regime have this choice completely removed. There are no choices to be made:

> For example, when a person is "faced with the alternative of betraying and thus murdering his friends or of sending his wife and children . . . to their death; when even suicide would mean the immediate murder of his own family," the very possibility of choosing good is removed.[7]

In short, *it was impossible to be a martyr in Auschwitz.*

In step three of the process of radical evil, "*any remaining trace of uniqueness, individuality, and spontaneity must be totally removed.* Spontaneity is for Arendt the mere possibility of doing something that cannot be simply and completely explained on the basis of reactions to the environment and preceding events."[8] Radical evil destroys spontaneity and in so doing annihilates the very essence of humanness. The idea of humanity becomes superfluous. So, when we talk about *a crime against humanity*, we are not merely talking about bad things happening to people. *Radical evil destroys the very idea of humanity.*

This kind of radical evil is not of course confined to totalitarian regimes. It is a dynamic that can be seen to varying degrees, in various situations where human beings: a) are in a position of power in which they assume they are right, and the other is wholly wrong; b) seek to justify barbarism by ensuring that "the other" is seen as something altogether different from and less than the rest of humanity; c) believe that no one is watching.

Here we might think of the atrocities committed in Abu Grebe during the Iraq war, the injustices of the American detention camp for suspected terrorists Guantanamo Bay, the colonial Belgian treatment of Africans, the Serbian rape camps, South African Apartheid, British and American slavery, . . . and the list goes on. All of these situations contain elements of radical evil—the killing of the juridical, moral, and spontaneous self—and

7. Formosa, "Is Radical Evil Banal?," 718.
8. Formosa, "Is Radical Evil Banal?," 719. (Italics added)

some of them contain all of the elements. Our brief foray into the darkness of pornography in chapter 2 indicates that it is not enough simply to write these things off as things that are done by "evil people" "somewhere else." *All of us* can knowingly or otherwise become involved with and become programmed by radical evil, even if it is simply a matter of saying nothing, doing nothing, not noticing, or looking the other way.

Radical evil and the strangeness of morality

There is one dimension of radical evil that we need to spend some time reflecting on before engaging with the Rwandan genocide. *Evil has a moral dimension.* Arendt was surprised that Eichmann was not some kind of amoral monster. She had expected him to be a man of few principles and little if any morality. However, it turned out that he (like all the creators of the Final Solution) had a strong moral dimension. It was just horribly distorted. If we are to understand the Rwandan genocide and its implications for today, we must first understand something of this moral dimension that accompanies radical evil.

The root causes of radical evil are always complex. However, there is a common thread that frequently runs through horrendous acts of violence on a personal and political level: *the perpetrators always think that they are right!* This is an important point bearing in mind what we discussed in chapter 1 regarding the connection between evil, misperception, and distorted thinking. The issue is not that people *lose* their morality. It is very often the exact opposite. *People become overly moral.* Arguing against the idea that dehumanization is necessary for violence to be perpetrated on another human being,[9] the psychologist Tage Rai writes:

> Across practices, across cultures, and throughout historical periods, when people support and engage in violence, their primary motivations are moral. By "moral," I mean that people are violent because they

9. Livingstone Smith, *Less Than Human: Why We Demean, Enslave, and Exterminate Others.*

> feel they must be; because they feel that their violence is obligatory. They know that they are harming fully human beings. Nonetheless, they believe they should. Violence does not stem from a psychopathic lack of morality. Quite the reverse: it comes from the exercise of perceived moral rights and obligations.[10]

The committing of a violent act is not necessarily the product of dehumanization, psychopathy, sadism, disinhibition, power, or greed (although any or all of these things may be involved). Rather, it is often *a moral act* within which people assume that they are doing what is right, just, and moral. Sometimes people even think that God is on their side. This of course should not come as a surprise to us. In chapter 1 we saw that for Paul, the primary problem for human beings lies in their "failure to acknowledge *God*, name *God as God*, and accept that God cannot be reduced to the self."[11] If we don't do this, we cannot read the world accurately. We become disoriented from God and start to think that good is evil and evil is good. This moral substitution of self for God is the essence of sin and the beginning point for evil.

Persuasion

Morality—those principles and assumptions that allow one to discern right from wrong—is not something that appears from nowhere. It is something that we learn and something that we are *persuaded* to accept. Human beings have a capacity to lead and to be led in the direction of both good and evil. When mass evil comes into existence it is always mobilized by powerful leaders who are able to persuade people that their cause is worth fighting for, dying for, torturing for, raping for, murdering for. These voices mobilize people by instilling compelling moral causes, derogating others, invoking historical grievances, and naming

10. Rai, "How Could They? Some People Are Ruthless. Some Lose Control. Yet Most Violence Remains Unfathomable. A New Theory Lights Up the Darkness." For an expansion on this perspective, see Rai, *Virtuous Violence*.

11. Eastman, "Empire of Illusion," 5.

enemies in ways that call into question their trustworthiness and value: cockroaches, rats, asylum seekers, thugs, blacks, whites, welfare queens, wetbacks, and so on. Importantly, *such leaders have to persuade people that what some might have previously thought was evil is in fact good.* The best way to mobilize ordinary people to carry out and support extraordinary acts of violence is to persuade them that these acts are not in fact evil at all. For example, Daniel Goldhagen highlights the bombing of Hiroshima and Nagasaki as morally ambiguous. He says that President Truman gave orders to annihilate

> the Japanese of Hiroshima and Nagasaki for . . . not entirely clear, reasons: perhaps his belief that it was a just way to hasten the war's end (even if, as Truman knew, the slaughter was not necessary to end the war soon), or perhaps to demonstrate American power to the Soviets for the emerging cold war struggle. But these different explanations do not make one slaughter a mass murder and the other not.[12]

Goldhagen's point is that *explaining* something is not the same thing as *justifying* it morally. There may have been good explanations as to why these cities were bombed, but such explanations do not get around the moral ambiguity of the act. In order for it to be framed as a just act, and for Truman not to be considered a war criminal, people had to be persuaded that it was the *right* thing to do, despite the ambiguity. The important point here being that *it is the winners and the powerful who get to determine the morality of the act.* I would imagine that there are few people in Japan today who think that the bombing of the two cities was a morally good action.

In times of conflict, each side assumes that its violent actions are "clearly" necessary in order that good can prevail. Sadly, the history of Christianity is not immune from this kind of moralized violence. Goldhagen writes,

12. Goldhagen, *Worse Than War*, 8.

> In the Jewish Bible, God instructs the ancient Jews to slaughter the peoples living in the "promised" land of ancient Israel. In the medieval world, mass murders were common, which the perpetrators often consecrated by invoking God. In the name of their Lord, Christian Crusaders slaughtered Jews, Muslims, and others in the eleventh and twelfth centuries. This age's greatest butchers were probably Genghis Khan and the Mongols, who killed peoples over vast terrain in Asia and Eastern Europe in the thirteenth century. In early modern and modern times imperial European peoples slaughtered many less technologically advanced peoples of other continents. In our time virtually all manner of peoples have perpetrated mass murder against virtually all kinds of victims.[13]

In each situation the aggressors assumed they were right, and that God was "clearly" on their side.

Creating distorted consciousness

In line with Eastman's analysis of Paul laid out in chapter 1, leaders have to find a way of creating a distorted consciousness in people in which they lose sight of what previously they may have assumed to be good, and substitute evil for that good in a way that makes them feel morally comfortable. Claudia Koonz in her book *The Nazi Conscience* notes that:

> Obscene though it might seem, Hitler's success derived from his ability to portray his policies as a moral project: reinstating German purity in the face of a Jewish enemy. The same logic of defending a virtuous ingroup against its imagined enemies was used to justify Stalin's terror. It continues to be used today by Islamic State as well as domestic terrorists in justifying violence.[14]

13. Goldhagen, *Worse Than War*, 19.
14. Koonz, *The Nazi Conscience*, 166.

Once *we* are placed in the "virtuous" position of assuming that we are completely right, it doesn't take much to suggest that *they* are completely wrong, and indeed are a danger to the goodness we seek to achieve. It's not that people are unaware of the harm that they cause: the issue is that they think it is "the right thing to do." So,

> In many instances, perpetrators are fully aware and they commit great harm—but do so only to the extent that they believe they are serving a higher purpose. Indeed, particularly shrill calls to throw everything at some great cause, whether that be a nation at war or the advancement of science, should arguably themselves be interpreted as a warning sign that trouble is on the way.[15]

It is our duty to recognize the dangers of this moral dynamic within evil and to read the signs in relation to what is going on around us.

Christians are not exempt from such dangerous morality. The genocide has particular poignance in that it was carried out by Christians on other Christians. Rwanda was the most successfully evangelized country in Africa. If an essential aspect of the gospel is loving your neighbor, avoiding temptation, and not being led into evil, what could have gone so horribly wrong?

Losing Faith in Humans: The Tragedy of Rwanda

The genocide

There is a story of a French priest in Rwanda who survived the massacres in 1994. He was asked whether his experiences of the genocide had shaken his faith in God. "Absolutely not," he replied. "But," he added matter-of-factly, "what happened in this country has destroyed my faith in mankind forever."[16]

The genocide in Rwanda was carried out with unimaginable savagery and cruelty. In a mere one hundred days, Hutus killed at

15. Reicher, Haslam, and Van Bavel, "How the Stanford Prison Experiment Gave Us the Wrong Idea about Evil."

16. Rieff, "God and Man in Rwanda."

least 800,000 African Tutsis, not with weapons of mass destruction, but with machetes and farming tools. They hacked them to death, chopped them in pieces, buried them in pits, dumped them in rivers. The killing was brutal and intimate. "In the Rwandan jails, one can find people who unblinkingly admit to having killed babies and old men with clubs or their bare hands, to setting fire to people as they huddled in church vestries, or to drowning pregnant women in streams."[17] Most of the killers were not military or militia, but ordinary people who had previously lived in harmony with the neighbors whom they killed. John Rucyahana in his book *The Bishop of Rwanda: Finding Forgiveness amidst a Pile of Bones* narrates some of the harrowing details:

> The amount of force applied to get them to kill varied greatly from village to village, but in some cases the government's official story of a spontaneous movement to kill the Tutsi was true. This was the result of years of indoctrination that began with the Belgians. Although the peasants often had to be pushed into carrying out the massacres, once they began, the suppressed resentments sprang forth into a terrifying full-blown hatred.[18]

Even young people and children were caught up as perpetrators of horror:

> While many of the killers in Kigali were young, the killers in the villages were even younger. Children as young as ten years old were given machetes and told to do their duty, which sometimes meant murdering their former playmates. In one village the children were given the head of one of their Tutsi classmates to use as a soccer ball. Killing was often a family affair. Mothers with babies on their backs killed other mothers who also carried babies on their backs—with little hesitation or doubt that what they were doing might be wrong.[19]

17. Rieff, "God and Man in Rwanda."
18. Rucyahana, *The Bishop of Rwanda*, 97.
19. Rucyahana, *The Bishop of Rwanda*, 98.

The mass killing was brutal, but it was not random. It was highly organized and had been planned for a long time. The assassination of the Rwandan president Juvénal Habyarimana was the match that lit the touch paper, but people had been well primed and well-armed before that.

According to the writer and political analyst David Rieff, contrary to the common Western assumption, the Rwandan genocide was not an act that emerged from historical tribal rivalry. By 1994, the Hutus and the Tutsis were not in fact different tribes. Writing in *Vanity Fair* Rieff observes:

> To the contrary, when the militias of the hard-line Hutu nationalist parties set upon their Tutsi neighbors—Hutu and Tutsi, though usually described as distinct tribes, and sometimes as different races, are historically as much castes as ethnic groups—the genocide they carried out had been long planned by their leaders. Even the brutal way the killing was done had a carefully conceived purpose. People are so predisposed to thinking of Africans as savages that few paused to ask themselves why much of the killing was done with machetes, clubs, and iron bars. But they wanted to do more than kill. Unlike Nazi Germany, where, for all the talk of collective guilt, the killing was done by a small group in death camps set out of sight of the general population, the Hutu leadership wanted to implicate as many citizens as possible. The "artisanal" nature of the violence was a way of creating a nation of accomplices in genocide. That, rather than any manipulation by militant radio broadcasts, was why so many Rwandans fled to Tanzania and Zaire when the Tutsi-led guerrillas of the Rwandan Patriotic Front (RPF) reconquered the country. Too many people had been willing or forced to participate in the killings—at least 100,000, by many estimates—for guilt to be fobbed off on neighbors or a few cadres of the old regime.[20]

If everyone is guilty, no one is guilty.

20. Rieff, "God and Man in Rwanda."

The response of the West

Following the genocide, there was a mass exodus of people to neighboring Zambia. This resulted in the formation of huge refugee camps that were full of violence and diseases such as cholera. The plight of people in the camps caught the attention of the West, who sent money and aid workers to help alleviate the suffering. What people watching the horrible scenes on their television sets did not realize was the reason why people had left Rwanda when the country was reconquered by the Tutsi-led forces. Many of the refugees were people who had killed, maimed, and raped their neighbors. They were fleeing possible repercussions from the Rwandan Patriotic Front. Likewise, people in the West didn't seem to consider that the cholera that was causing so much suffering may have been caused by living with multiple dead bodies.

The irony of this situation is compounded by the fact that the initial reaction of the West when the genocide began was to withdraw all its people. So white businessmen, missionaries, clergy, and entrepreneurs were all rushed out of the country leaving their Rwandan co-workers to be killed. Westerners who had worked closely with and had been dependant on Rwandans simply left them to their fate. Bill Clinton and his administration refused to use the term genocide or to intervene, something for which he later apologized.[21] The United Nations refused to send the minimal number of troops that would have been necessary to stop the killings. The United Nations soldiers who were there were not allowed to intervene, despite protestation and multiple requests to allow its soldiers to help. The people of Rwanda were simply left to their fate. After the genocide, the West seemed keen to help. However, it was during the genocide that people had needed help. "By the time the C-130s began landing in Kigali again, the slaughter was over. It had ended because the R.P.F. had been victorious on the battlefield, not because the world was any better at stopping genocide in 1994 than it had been in 1944."[22]

21. Hughes, "Bill Clinton Regrets Rwanda Now (Not So Much in 1994)."
22. Rieff, "God and Man in Rwanda."

The role of the church

One of the most troubling aspects of the Rwandan genocide was the role that the church and its clergy played in the killings. Timothy Longman in his paper on the role of the Christian church in the Rwandan genocide notes that in terms of the role of religion, Rwanda was unique, though, he reminds us,

> that religious institutions should be implicated in a genocide is not exceptional. In Rwanda, however, unlike the genocides of Armenians in Turkey, Jews in Europe in World War II, and Muslims in Bosnia, and to the genocidal violence between Hindus, Muslims, and Sikhs in India and Christians and various Muslim groups in Lebanon, religion did not serve as an ascriptive identifier to demarcate a social group as an essential "other." Both Catholic and Protestant churches in Rwanda are multi-ethnic, and the genocide in Rwanda occurred within religious groups. In most communities members of a church parish killed their fellow parishioners and even, in a number of cases, their own pastor or priest.[23]

In other genocides, it was people's religion that marked out a particular group as the enemy to be feared and destroyed. This was not the case in Rwanda. It was not religious identities that were at stake here. It was ethnic and national identity that were the dividing lines. Longman continues:

> The church was implicated in the genocide in numerous ways. People who sought sanctuary in church buildings were instead slaughtered there. According to some estimates, more people were killed in church buildings than anywhere else. At one parish where I researched, the communal mayor reports that 17,000 bodies were unearthed from one set of latrines alongside the church. Numerous Tutsi priests, pastors, brothers, and nuns were killed, often by their own parishioners, sometimes by their fellow clergy. While the failure of the population to respect the principle of sanctuary cannot be

23. Longman, "Christian Churches and Genocide in Rwanda."

> blamed on the churches, the failure of the church leadership to condemn massacres on church property and attacks on church personnel in the years preceding the genocide clearly undermined the principle of sanctuary in Rwanda.[24]

In the preceding years, the church worldwide had failed to condemn previous mass killings in the region, and indeed continued to remain largely silent as the genocide unfolded. This, combined with the highly visible withdrawal of Westerners from the country and the failure of the UN to intervene, meant that the killers basically had free rein not only to do what they wanted, but also to assume that the silence of the West and the silence of the church were signs of affirmation.

Many of the mass killings occurred in church buildings. General Roméo Dallaire was the commander of the UN troops in Rwanda. He was in a position to stop it early on, but was prevented from doing so by the UN, something that has had a devastating impact upon his mental health in the long term. In his book *Shake Hands with the Devil: The Failure of Humanity in Rwanda*, he recounts one of many massacres that occurred in church buildings, places that in other times and in other contexts would have been places of sanctuary:

> In the aisles and on the pews were bodies of hundreds of men, women, and children. At least fifteen of them were still alive but in a terrible state. The priests were applying first aid to the survivors. A baby cried as it tried to feed on the breast of its dead mother, . . . the two Polish MILOBs [Military Observers] . . . were in a state of grief and shock, hardly able to relate what had happened. The night before, they said, the RGF had cordoned off the area, and then the Gendarmerie had gone door to door checking identity cards. All Tutsi men, women, and children were rounded up and moved to the church. . . . Then the gendarmes welcomed in a large number of civilian militiamen with machetes and handed over the victims to their killers. Methodically and with much bravado and

24. Longman, "Christian Churches and Genocide in Rwanda."

> laughter, the militia moved from bench to bench, hacking with machetes. Some people died immediately, while others with terrible wounds begged for their lives or the lives of their children. No one was spared. A pregnant woman was disembowelled and her fetus severed. Women suffered horrible mutilation. Men were struck on the head and died immediately or lingered in agony. Children begged for their lives and received the same treatment as their parents. Genitalia were a favourite target, the victims left to bleed to death. There was no mercy, no hesitation, and no compassion. The priests and the MILOBs, guns at their throats, tears in their eyes, and the screams of the dying in their ears, pleaded with the gendarmes for the victims. The gendarmes' reply was to use the rifle barrels to lift the priests' and MILOBs' heads so that they could better witness the horror.[25]

Scenes like this could be multiplied literally thousands of times. Worse, pastors sometime led their flocks into their churches fully aware that the people would be killed. There is even an example of two nuns who were convicted of supplying the gasoline that set fire to a church killing hundreds of people.[26] If we wanted living proof as to what radical evil looks like and what it does on a grand scale, the Rwandan genocide is one place (sadly not the only place) where it seems crystal clear. When the power of radical evil takes over politics, religion, communities, and individuals unspeakable things happen.

The failure of Christian practices

Recently there has been some important research done into why it is that Christian practices do not always succeed in forming people in the ways they intend.[27] This observation—that Christian practices can be ambiguous in their practical outcomes—finds a powerful embodiment in the context of the killings in Rwanda.

25. Dallaire, quoted in Rucyahana, *The Bishop of Rwanda*, 77–78.
26. Ames, "Two Rwandan Nuns Convicted of War Crimes."
27. Winner, *The Dangers of Christian Practice*.

Remember that Rwanda was a heavily evangelized country and church attendance and participation in the rituals and practices of the church were extensive. The Rwandan killers had at their fingertips all of the spiritual gifts that Scripture informs us we need to resist and to overcome evil (Eph 6:10–20). And yet those who killed chose not only not to put on the spiritual armor of God but actually *to take it off* in order to kill.

In his book *Machete Season: The Killers in Rwanda Speak*, the journalist Jean Hatzfeld presents a harrowing picture of the genocide through interviews with those who killed. The killers talk about going out hunting for Tutsis for eight hours every day, about killing until they were exhausted, cutting the Achilles' tendons of those whom they hadn't the time to kill so that they could not escape, going home for food and sleep, and then returning the next day to finish the job. Their wives sometimes scolded them for overdoing things. In the section of the book titled "and God in all of this?" the killers discuss how they felt about God when they were killing. Adalbert, one of the killers says this:

> The Saturday after the plane crash was the usual choir rehearsal day at the church in Kibungo. We sang hymns in good feeling with our Tutsi compatriots, our voices still blending in chorus. On Sunday morning we returned at the appointed hour for mass; they did not arrive. They had already fled into the bush in fear of reprisals, driving their goats and cows before them. This disappointed us greatly, especially on a Sunday. Anger hustled us outside the church door. We left the Lord and our prayers inside to rush home. We changed from our Sunday best into our workday clothes, we grabbed clubs and machetes, we went straight off killing.[28]

Ignace, another killer says this:

> The white priests took off at the first skirmishes. The black priests joined the killers or the killed. God kept silent, and the churches stank from abandoned bodies. Religion could not find its place in our activities. For a little

28. Hatzfeld, *Machete Season*, 140.

> while, we were no longer ordinary Christians, we had to forget our duties learned in catechism class. We had first of all to obey our leaders—and God only afterward, very long afterword, to make confession and penance. When the job was done.[29]

"For a little while, we were no longer Christians." These are deeply troubling words. Instead of putting on the armor of God and resisting evil, they put their spiritual armor to one side and followed the bidding of the state until the job was done. How could this happen?

The issue of identity

There are complex political, economic, and historical elements that set the scene for the genocide in Rwanda. However, there is one vital theological and social dimension that is of crucial importance for current purposes and that is the issue of *Christian identity*. Emmanuel Katongole conceives of this point as central to understanding what went on during and before the genocide. Katongole points out that the Rwandan genocide was not a form of ethnic or tribal violence:

> whatever role the categories of Hutu and Tutsi played in pre-colonial Rwanda, they cannot be reasonably referred to as "tribes" or "ethnicities." For not only did Hutu and Tutsi speak the same language, they shared the same culture, same religious traditions, lived on the same hills, and were greatly intermarried. In fact, as Philip Gourevitch points out, prior to European colonialism, "there are few people in Europe among whom one finds these three factors of national cohesion: one language, one faith, one law."[30]

Hutu and Tutsi were not biological, racial, or cultural differences, they were *political identities* (shaped in view of a future political

29. Hatzfeld, *Machete Season*, 86.

30. Katongole, *The Journey of Reconciliation*; quoting Gourevitch, *We Wish to Inform You That Tomorrow We Will Be Killed with Our Families*, 55.

project) that were formed within the political and colonial history of Rwanda.

> *Cultural identities* reflect something of the past (a shared history, language, customs, beliefs, etc.), whereas *"political" identities* are in view of a future political project: They are a direct consequence of the history of state formation, and not of market or cultural formation. If economic identities are a consequence of the history of development of markets, and cultural identities of the development of communities that share a common language and meaning, political identities need to be understood as a specific consequence of the history of state formation. When it comes to the modern state, political identities are inscribed in law. In the first instance, they are legally enforced.[31]

The development of the political identities of Hutus and Tutsis was fuelled by a complex colonial and religious history that sought to use, create, and employ division for the furtherance of political or ecclesial power. Katongole traces the theological dimensions of these political identities to the nineteenth-century missionary work in Africa:

> Shaped within an Enlightenment context, nineteenth-century missionary work by and large assumed and operated out of a neo-scholastic grace vs. nature distinction according to which mission (the church's competence) was located within an essentially "spiritual" realm, thus surrendering the "natural" sphere to the realm of politics. And thus, even when evangelization met with great success, as the case of Rwanda confirms, it was simply assumed that the church's role was primarily spiritual and pastoral. Accordingly, the church never understood herself as competent or even able to provide an alternative configuration of Rwandan society in terms of a distinct Christian anthropology beyond the

31. Mamdani, *When Victims Become Killers*, 22.

> notions of "Hutu" and "Tutsi," which had by now come to be accepted as "natural" identities.[32]

The church was so identified with the nation state that it had no capacity or desire to produce theologies that challenged the overarching political and racial narrative. Religion was significant, but it contained a type of spirituality that was dislocated from material things and, as such, played only a tangential role in identity formation. The problem then was one of formation, or more accurately, of the *lack of formation of a Christian identity*. People knew and engaged with the practices of the faith—they prayed, sang, worshipped—but such practices were not central to their *identity*. It was the state that provided their primary identity.

Katongole suggests that the

> overall effect of this "religious" outlook of Christianity is not only an exaggerated deference to the so-called "natural" categories of "race," "tribe," or "ethnicity." It is to seal off these notions from any radical theological reconfiguration.[33] This is what turns these so called "natural" identities into rich fodder for ideological manipulation within the violent politics of post-colonial Africa.[34]

It is true that Rwanda was successfully evangelized in terms of numbers, but it is also true that Christian identity was usurped by people's political and ethnic identities. This is at least partly because the mission strategy of the church was to target the powerful and then to get powerful leaders to convince their people to convert. Within such an approach, the idea of thoughtfulness or individuals engaging in critical thinking was simply not available. People were thus shaped and formed by powerful forces that prevented them from developing the ability to think clearly about what the situation actually was, and who was and who was not to be considered their enemy. When it came to the act of

32. Katongole, *The Journey of Reconciliation*, Kindle loc 1822–23.

33. Mamdani, *When Victims Become Killers*, 99.

34. Katongole, *The Journey of Reconciliation*, Kindle loc 1839.

genocide, people were wholly convinced that what they were doing was the right thing to do.

Combine this with the work of the Rwandan media, which constantly put forth radio propaganda telling the Hutus that the Tutsis were the enemy—cockroaches—who were going to kill them and take their land, and you can see how the scene was set. The banality of evil is well illustrated by the fact that someone's perspective can be so completely transformed by simply listening to a barrage of messages on the radio that they become primed to kill. (Contemporary social media users might be wise to see the warning here.) Understood in this light, the statement by the Rwandan killer mentioned earlier begins to make sense: "We had first of all to obey our leaders—and God only afterward, very long afterwards, to make confession and penance. When the job was done." Once again, we come back to the apostle Paul's claim that the problem with people is their "failure to acknowledge God, name God as God, and accept that God cannot be reduced to the self." What we see here is distorted thinking, mistaken morality, and cognitive confusion on a mass scale.

Lessons from Rwanda: cultural identity

Is there anything to be learned from this horrendous evil? The answer is yes, and I think it is crucial that the lessons are learned. We saw earlier that for Katongole the issue of Christian identity was a central feature in the history and outworking of the genocide. The issue of identity is a highly contentious issue for modern people, particularly within the West. We can see this in the various movements and slogans that have driven our politics in recent times:

- Trump: Make America great again!
- Brexit: "Take back control" of our country!—you are either a "leaver" or a "remainer"!
- Black lives matter! White lives matter! All lives matter!
- If you don't vote Democrat, you're not black!

- The pandemic: maskers and unmaskers; vaxers or anti-vaxers
- Trans identities
- Non-binary identities

The issue of identity is at the forefront of a good deal of contemporary debate and confusion. People are searching deeply for identity and ultimately a place of belonging. Many of us assume identity to be a personal choice. But of course, when identity is perceived as a personal choice that immediately opens us up to those powerful forces within society that seek to shape and form our "personal" choices. We may *think* we are choosing, but very often we are actually subtly being told what to do.

Today in the West we have so much choice that we often can't see the manipulations of the powers that shape and form us. We think we are choosing who we want to be, but you just have to spend a few hours on social media to know that we are constantly being shaped and formed by forces outside of our own choices. The current tendency to "cancel" people if they express beliefs that are different from the majority view is an example of the ambiguity of free speech and choice and the power of majorities. Evil likes to separate us, categorize us, polarize us, and turn us against one another. It confuses our worldly identities with our identity in Jesus, seeking to divide us into separate camps of hatred from whence evil and division will inevitably flow. When we split into separate camps, we can't help but see the other as "the evil one."

We can see this kind of dynamic at work in the kind of polarizing identity politics that goes on inside and outside of the church. It lurks behind conversations around who is black and who is white, who is male and who is female, who is gay and who is straight, American and non-American, British and non-British. Of course, "we" always think that "our" camp is right. And herein lies the problem. If "we" are right, then everyone else *must be* wrong, and our personal opinions become the only arbitrators of the truth. This is precisely the kind of situation that Paul described in Romans. People turn themselves over to false gods who provide false identities and confuse them about what is good and what is evil, what is of God and what is evil.

Paul is very clear that we do not find our identity in the places where we might "naturally" think our identities should lie. In Galatians 3:28 Paul reminds us that, "There is neither Jew nor Greek, neither slave nor free, nor is there male and female, for you are all one in Christ Jesus." *Our beginning point for discovering* (rather than simply choosing) *our identity lies as we find ourselves bound together within the body of Jesus.* Within that body, diversity in unity is the norm. Certainly, we are called to fight for justice, equality, fairness, and truth. However, we are also called to love our enemies and bless those who curse us.

Our Christian identity thus complexifies our dealings with the world and our negotiating of our other necessary but secondary identities. It refuses to allow the dichotomizing work of sin to polarize us in such a way that we begin to see evil only in the other and rarely within ourselves. Our Christian identity respects our other sources of identity—race, culture, religion, sexuality, gender, and so forth—and seeks after justice in these areas, but always in relation to and according to the parameters of our Christian identity: *unity in diversity is our new norm.*

This calls for theological humility and a recognition that evil is within as well as out with ourselves. If we find ourselves hating a perceived enemy because of their color, sexuality, culture, or nationality, then we know that we have lost sight of who we are in Christ. Finding our identity in Christ prevents us from allowing other identities to lead us into temptation and confusion. Accepting our identity in Christ is the first step in delivering us from evil. Other identities are important, but none of them surpasses our primary identity in Christ. There can never be a time when we put our Christian identity to one side until the job is done, whether that job involves our work, our money, our vote, or the modus operandi of our political action. Our Christian identity requires discernment and critical thinking about ourselves, others, and the world, a lack of which, as we have seen, Hannah Arendt locates as a profound source of evil.

The evil of doing nothing

Finding our identity in Christ and thus not being led into temptation and evil may be the gospel. But the question is, do we live it out? One of the most challenging questions that emerges from the Rwandan genocide is whether Christian identity actually matters *in practice*. We know the theory, but do we actually live it out? It's easy for us to answer this question too quickly. But listen again to Katongole here, who notes,

> Maybe the deepest tragedy of the Rwandan genocide is that Christianity didn't seem to make any difference. Rwandans performed a script that had shaped them more deeply than the biblical story had. Behind the silences of genocide, Hutus and Tutsis alike were shaped by a story that held their imaginations captive. Paying attention to history helps us to see that this was not just Rwanda's problem. The story that made Rwanda is the story of the West. When we look at Rwanda as a mirror to the church, it helps us realize what little consequence the biblical story has on the way Christians live their lives in the West. As Christians, we cannot remember the Rwandan genocide without admitting that the gospel did not seem to have a real impact on most Rwandans' lives. Seeing this, we have to ask: does Christianity make any real difference in the West? The question is not so much whether Jesus' message has been proclaimed in all the earth. The real question is, what difference has the gospel made in people's lives?[35]

What a challenge! But he is right. Why is it that we Christians seem quite comfortable that huge amounts of food from supermarkets is simply discarded each day when each day 25,000 people, including more than 10,000 children, die from hunger and related causes?[36] Supermarkets have become a sign of our great abundance. But is this how God desires God's abundance to be shared? Why is it that

35. Katongole and Wilson-Hartgrove, *Mirror to the Church*, 85.

36. Holmes, "Losing 25,000 to Hunger Every Day" (accessed August 25, 2021).

there are black churches and white churches if all divisions have been broken down in Jesus? Why is it that I have two cars when my neighbor a few doors down or a few miles away from me has none? Or even has no home? How does this fit in with Jesus's command to love our neighbors and to share what we have with the poor? Why is it that there is not an ecclesiological outcry that drives Christians on to the streets when the UK government slashes its foreign aid, thus sentencing thousands of people to deeper poverty and possible death? Why are Christians relatively silent on the genocide that is currently taking place amongst God's people? Katongole sums up the issue in this way:

> What I cannot understand or accept as a Christian minister is the fact that the church rarely offers a different story. I refuse to accept the assumption that all Christianity has to offer is insight about how to secure and enjoy the "blessings" of our global economy. Yes, Christians continue to read the Bible and preach the gospel in the West. But prayer, Bible study, and Christian language easily become a gloss for people who are most decidedly shaped by something else. It's too easy for Christianity to have no consequence in our world.[37]

This challenge is profound. Perhaps it is time for a self-audit that checks to see if we (all of us together) are actually living the gospel and living into our Christian identities, or whether we are in fact shaped by other stories, other powers. Clearly, Christian identity meant very little to those who engaged in genocidal activities. But before we become overly judgmental, perhaps it is time to look at *ourselves* in what Katongole calls the mirror of Rwanda. We may not like what we see.

"Wait a minute!" you may say. "I get the point, and maybe we do need to see through some of these illusions. But at least we are not guilty of genocide! And what do you mean that Christians are relatively silent on the genocide that is currently taking place amongst God's people. What genocide?" These are fair comments, so allow me to explain what I mean.

37. Katongole and Wilson-Hartgrove, *Mirror to the Church*, 87.

The Persecution of the Christian Church

The Rwandan genocide was wholly preventable. As we have seen, the West could have intervened, and the killing could have been prevented. The evil of inaction was apparent. This is a powerful warning. When the church is silent, evil flourishes. As the writer of Proverbs puts it:

> Rescue those who are unjustly sentenced to die; save them as they stagger to their death. Don't excuse yourself by saying, "Look, we didn't know." For God understands all hearts, and he sees you. He who guards your soul knows you knew. He will repay all people as their actions deserve. (Prov 24:11–12, NLT)

This passage is a powerful warning that brings us back to the issue I raised in the introduction to this book: *our awareness of and response to (or often our lack of awareness of and response to) Christian persecution.* Damian Thompson writing in *The Spectator* outlines what religious persecution looks like in 2019:

- The rape, murder, and dismemberment of pregnant Christian women in Nigeria by Islamist thugs.
- The use of face-recognition technology by the Chinese government to monitor, control, and, where it deems necessary, eradicate Christian worship by demolishing thousands of churches.
- The evisceration of ancient Christian communities in the lands of the Bible.
- The relentless torture of Christians in North Korea.
- The burning of Christian villages by Hindu nationalists in India, and vicious attacks on Christians in Sri Lanka and Burma by Buddhists, egged on by bloodthirsty monks. It's hard to overestimate the threat to religious freedom posed by the spread of Asian religious nationalism.[38]

38. Thompson, "Why Liberals Turn a Blind Eye to the Global Persecution of Christians."

Thompson concludes: "Meanwhile the Church of England builds helter-skelters and crazy golf courses in its cathedrals, while the Vatican is manoeuvred by Beijing into signing a concordat that legitimizes China's government-run parody of the Catholic Church. It's a scandalous situation."[39]

The gravity of the issue and the church's apparent relative lack of interest or lack of awareness is painful. The evidence for Christian persecution is chilling. Thompson's conclusion is sobering.

But there is more.

The Truro Report

In 2019, the then Foreign Secretary of the UK government Jeremy Hunt commissioned the Anglican Bishop of Truro, Rt. Rev. Philip Mounstephen, to provide an independent review on the persecutions of Christians across the world.[40] His findings were shocking. He found widespread evidence that Christians are by far the most widely persecuted religion and that religious persecution is a growing phenomenon globally. "Approximately 245 million Christians suffer high levels of persecution or worse—30 million up on the previous year."[41] The Bishop of Truro's report equates what is going on as a mode of genocide. The report makes the stark observation that "The main impact of such genocidal acts against Christians is exodus. Christianity now faces the possibility of being wiped-out in parts of the Middle East." . . . Where these and other incidents meet the test of genocide, governments will be required to bring perpetrators to justice, aid victims, and take preventative measures for the future." Genocide is an intention. You don't have to be totally successful in order to be engaging in it.

The British government has promised to implement the findings of the Report. But that was before the pandemic. It would

39. Thompson, "Why Liberals Turn a Blind Eye to the Global Persecution of Christians."

40. The Bishop of Truro's Independent Review for the UK Foreign Secretary of Foreign and Commonwealth Office Support for Persecuted Christians.

41. Release International, "Persecution of Christians 'Close to Genocide.'"

be very easy for the abuse of our brothers and sisters in Christ to be forgotten about as we enter into this new world of economic struggle and rebuilding of communities and relationships. If the genocidal evil of Christian persecution is to be resisted, we need to make sure that it is kept firmly on people's personal and political horizons. If we do nothing or if we wait until things "get better," we simply encourage evil doers to do more evil. If we are genuine in our cry of "never again!" then each one of us must pick up the responsibility to pray and act in support of the persecuted body of Jesus. As we begin to construct the new norm, we need to take very seriously the doctrine of the Body of Christ and realize that the presence of radical evil is not happening "somewhere else," in another place and time, but within the very body in which we claim to be participating as faithful followers of Jesus. Radical evil is a reality in which all of us participate, knowingly or otherwise. Silence is participation. If we are to resist such evil, we need to learn how to see it.

We should bear in mind William Wilberforce's speech to the House of Commons concerning the slave trade in 1791 that opens the Truro report: "You may choose to look the other way, but you can never again say that you did not know."

Conclusion: Christian Identity, Awareness, Critical Thinking, and Political Action

In this chapter we have explored some pretty tough subjects. The Rwandan genocide was horrible, unnecessary, and wholly preventable. The theological dynamics that I have tried to draw out here remind us of our own responsibilities to prevent great evils like genocide, but also to be aware of the deep evils within our own contexts that can lead to similar situations. We have looked at the practices of *Christian identity formation, critical thinking*, and *faithful political action*. In the closing chapter of this book, we will return to some of these themes and begin to respond to the question: *what kind of people must we be to recognise and resist evil?*

4

Countering Evil

What Kind of People Do We Need to Be to Recognize and Resist Evil?

It should be clear by now that evil is a complex and pervasive phenomenon in which we are all caught up, knowingly or otherwise. Reflection on the pandemic has brought to light some important aspects of the banality of evil. It has also moved us to consider the issue of radical evil. The connection between the pandemic and the rise of strident and divisive right-wing politics should serve as a warning that all of us could quite easily get caught up in situations where we find ourselves drawn into evil. As soon as people start talking about "migrants" instead of people who are the victims of war, we know that we are moving in a dangerous direction. Our reflection on Rwanda helps us to realize that the people of Rwanda were not moral monsters. They were ordinary people who mistook their identity in Christ for their identity in the nation state. As importantly, the role of the West historically and contemporarily indicates that responsibility for radical evil is not confined to those who engage in particular "front line" actions. Genocide requires the participation of systems and powers, sometimes many miles away from the locus of the situation. We would do well to examine ourselves and our own contexts to see which powers and influences are at work in our own lives and the lives or our communities. If silence and an unwillingness to intervene are modes of evil, then ultimately, we will discover that we too are perpetrators both of banal and of radical evil.

In order to resist evil, we need to become the kind of people who can both recognize evil and know how to resist it. We have already begun to see how theological reflection on key issues can draw our attention to vital dimensions of the process of discernment and action—such things as *faith, hope, love, trust, generosity, thoughtfulness, neighborliness,* and *Christian identity*. These insights and practices are the everyday spiritual weapons that are ours through our participation in the work of the Spirit. As we engage with the Spirit, we are enabled to see evil and resist temptation and remain open to and aware of the need for God's deliverance. The issue of God's deliverance is crucial. There is only so much that we as human beings can do in our battle against evil. Our struggle is certainly material. Evil manifests itself in human actions and aberrations. Nonetheless, on our own, it is not possible for us to resist such temptations, not least because sometimes, as we have seen, we struggle to even recognize them as temptations. As Paul puts it in Romans 7:15–20:

> I do not understand what I do. For what I want to do I do not do, but what I hate I do. And if I do what I do not want to do, I agree that the law is good. As it is, it is no longer I myself who do it, but it is sin living in me. For I know that good itself does not dwell in me, that is, in my sinful nature. For I have the desire to do what is good, but I cannot carry it out. For I do not do the good I want to do, but the evil I do not want to do—this I keep on doing. Now if I do what I do not want to do, it is no longer I who do it, but it is sin living in me that does it.

Living lives that can recognize and resist evil requires God's action. It is not a "by the way" that Jesus asks us to pray that we will be delivered from evil (Matt 6:13). In our own strength we cannot resist the temptation to do evil. But with God all things are possible (Matt 19:26). This takes us to the issue of spiritual warfare.

Powers and Principalities

In Colossians 1:15–20 Paul talks about powers and principalities:

> The Son is the image of the invisible God, the firstborn over all creation. For in him all things were created: things in heaven and on earth, visible and invisible, whether thrones or powers or rulers or authorities; all things have been created through him and for him. He is before all things, and in him all things hold together. And he is the head of the body, the church; he is the beginning and the firstborn from among the dead, so that in everything he might have the supremacy. For God was pleased to have all his fullness dwell in him, and through him to reconcile to himself all things, whether things on earth or things in heaven, by making peace through his blood, shed on the cross.

The idea of being influenced by forces beyond our control may at first appear somewhat anachronistic. We might be thinking: "Surely Paul is offering a pre-modern view. We don't believe in such things nowadays, do we?" It is true that the cosmology of Paul's time was in many ways quite different from our own. However, the language of the powers is in fact highly relevant for the contemporary world. Today we frequently talk about economic forces that cause mass redundancy, homelessness, poverty, and wealth inequalities. The power of war creates millions of refugees, which in turn challenges the power of the state to deal with them positively or negatively. During the 2020–21 pandemic, governments were given special powers to restrain the freedoms of their citizens. We couldn't *see* these powers, but if we tried to step outside, we certainly felt their consequences. The power of love and compassion drives people to sacrificial acts, which sometimes make very little logical sense. "Economic forces," "the political climate," "the market," "the power of democracy," "military power," "medical power" and the "healthcare system," "institutional racism," "systems of dictatorship": the list goes on. We saw that it was historical, religious, and political powers, along with the power of persuasion (something that seems to have superseded the desire for truth, honesty, and goodness within contemporary politics) that lay behind the Rwandan genocide. It is economic powers, the power of lust, and the power of human domination over other humans that drives the business of pornography. Social and political powers underpin the evils of sexism, homophobia, disablism, and every other human way of categorizing human beings that leads to unnecessary pain and suffering. And if we ask why millions of people are starving when this planet is perfectly capable of growing and distributing sufficient food for every man, woman, and child on it, the answer is the same: there are *forces* that stop us doing it. Forces and powers are all around us. We cannot touch and see these forces, but we can certainly see and feel their outcomes. Some of these powers may, for a while, come to be quite closely identified with certain human beings; but take that person away, and the force will remain.[1]

Of course, in the same way as we could explain away evil using psychological or sociological categories, we could simply explain away these powers and forces in political, economic, or sociological terms. Paul wants us to see that such explanations are not necessarily wrong, but they are inadequate. Politics, economics, sociology, and social psychology are important factors, but Paul urges us to see that there is something deep and dark that lurks behind such powers and forces: *malignant powers and principalities*. Paul helps us to notice these deeper dimensions of what the powers are doing and, importantly, what they *should* be doing. The powers were originally intended to serve God's good purposes. All things were made in Christ, through Christ, and for Christ (Col 1:16). What went wrong is similar to what we discovered in our exploration of evil and sin in the first chapter: human beings transferred their allegiance from God to the powers. As biblical scholar N. T. Wright puts it:

1. Wright, *Following Jesus*, 16.

> When humans refuse to use God's gift of sexuality responsibly, they are handing over their power to Aphrodite, and she will take control. When humans refuse to use God's gift of money responsibly, they are handing over their power to Mammon, and he will take control. And so on.[2]

As we think about the issues that we have looked at thus far—rejection of the vulnerable, greed, lack of generosity, fear of strangers, toxic politics, pornography, genocide, and lack of awareness and action in relation to Christian persecution—we can see this process of handing over power quite clearly. It doesn't have to be a deliberate thing. You just need not to think. Such alliances with the powers substitute God with self and deliberately or otherwise refuse to accept the truth or the true purposes to which the powers should be attuned. Inevitably when this happens human beings are deceived, crushed, and broken.

Victory in the Cross of Jesus

But all is not lost! Wright points out that:

> Jesus took on the principalities and powers. He lived, and taught, a way of being Israel, a way of being human, which challenged the powers at every point. The powers said you should live for money. Jesus said you can't serve God and Mammon. The powers said that Israel's path to liberation would come through the sword. Jesus said that those who take the sword will perish by the sword. The powers said that Caesar was Lord of the world. Jesus proclaimed the kingdom of God.[3]

The cross was not a defeat of Jesus at the hands of the powers, but the exact opposite. The powers were defeated through the resurrection of Jesus. The most that the powers can do is to kill someone. After that they are silent. But Jesus continues to speak

2. Wright, *Following Jesus*, 18.

3. Wright, *Following Jesus*, 18–19.

even after death, and in so doing puts the powers in their place. Importantly, in Jesus, the powers are *reconciled.* It is not that they are destroyed; they are defeated and put back in their rightful place. That is of course an ongoing movement, but noticing this is important in terms of the nature of our resistance. Ultimately Jesus is the one and only true deliverer. The battle against the powers is God's battle. Nevertheless, the powers reveal themselves in material systems and tangible principalities. If it is the case that the powers are defeated but still need to be re-ordered by the power of God's love, then the penultimate task of Christians is to engage in forms of peaceable spiritual warfare that challenge the powers to be what they were intended to be: *just, fair, kind, thoughtful, caring, faithful, worshipful,* and above all, *loving.*

Spiritual Warfare

This kind of engagement calls for a particular kind of spiritual warfare. The idea of spiritual warfare is complex and shifts and changes across traditions. Here I am using the term in the way that the theologian Richard Foster uses it in his essay: "The peaceable war of the lamb." Here Foster lays out some of the parameters of spiritual warfare:

> All who desire to follow Jesus are called into the peaceable war of the Lamb against all principalities and powers. Like any warfare, it is waged on all fronts at once—inward and outward, personal and social, individual and institutional. The perimeter of its concerns embraces three hundred sixty degrees. Inwardly the Lamb of God seeks to conquer all forms of pride, lust, greed, hate, fear, envy, and everything that stands against life in the kingdom of God. But Jesus, our conquering King, refuses to stop with the private sector of life. All kinds of injustice, oppression, hatred, bigotry, cruelty, tyranny, brutality, and anything else opposed to the way of God are legitimate battle grounds in this spiritual warfare.[4]

4. Foster, "The Peaceable War of the Lamb."

The weapons for such spiritual warfare are unusual in comparison with human warfare: prayer, faith, love, peace, truth, integrity (Ephesians 6). These are the ways in which we draw the sting of power's evil and step into the gap that God creates for us. These spiritual weapons are not simply against flesh and blood. They are "against the principalities, against the powers, against the world rulers of this present darkness, against the spiritual hosts of wickedness in the heavenly places" (Eph 6:12). This is not to imply any kind of spiritual dualism. Foster is clear on this point: "the aim of our attack is to defeat the principalities that control and incarnate themselves in flesh and blood."[5] The Lamb's war is not defined by flesh and blood, but it certainly involves them. Importantly,

> the warfare of the lamb is not social or political stance [sic]. Its aim is not even to correct societal ills. That is the result, to be sure, but almost never in the way in which we imagine it. The kingdom of our God and of his Christ is of another reality altogether, and while its effects are to pull down the kingdoms of this world, it does so only as a consequence of a deeper reality.[6]

Formation and action

There are two key dynamics that we need to bear in mind as we prepare for spiritual warfare: *formation* and *action*. There is an inward development—sanctification—by which the Spirit shapes us to mirror something of the life of Jesus and to live in Jesus's victory. There is a synchronous outward movement that recognizes God's ultimate victory over the powers and moves to challenge the powers in their spiritual (prayer, contemplation, discernment, and worship) and material dimensions (actions that reveal God's love, peace, fairness, and justice). Through this movement, we "overcome evil with good" (Rom 12:21). In the Lamb's war, Foster continues:

5. Foster, "The Peaceable War of the Lamb."
6. Foster, "The Peaceable War of the Lamb."

> we have an attack on evil in all its guises, overcoming it with good. There is brotherly love, radical sharing, witness without compromise, and an obedient, disciplined, freely gathered, martyr people who know in this life the life and power of the kingdom of God. Such people are committed in revolutionary faithfulness to Christ's everlasting rule in an eternal kingdom of peace, not only imminent on the horizon but already coming to birth in our midst.[7]

That deeper reality is the victory over the powers that Jesus wrought on the cross and it continues to be worked out in the ongoing movement of redemption into which all human beings are invited to enter and participate. Spiritual warfare is an active movement that strives to affirm that even in the midst of the most horrendous of evils and the deceptive sense that the powers of darkness are winning, there is a God who is working for change and who is worthy of worship.

The power of love: tough minds and tender hearts

The inspiration for the weapons of spiritual warfare is love. We worship a God who *is* love (1 John 4:8) and who promises love for the world (John 3:16). The calling of all of Christians is to love. The Trappist monk Thomas Merton puts it this way:

> Our job is to love others without stopping to inquire whether or not they are worthy. That is not our business and, in fact, it is nobody's business. What we are asked to do is to love, and this love itself will render both ourselves and our neighbors worthy.[8]

It is as we strive to love, that we do good. It is as we do good that we overcome evil: "Do not be overcome by evil but overcome evil with good" (Rom 12:21).

7. Foster, "The Peaceable War of the Lamb."

8. Letter to Dorothy Day, quoted in Hand, *Catholic Voices in a World on Fire*, 180.

Yet we must be clear about what we mean when we talk about love. Love is not just a romantic form of divinized niceness. Jesus's words in Matthew 10:16 make interesting reading in relation to how we should think about the practice of love. There, he rather enigmatically says: "I am sending you out like sheep among wolves. Therefore, be as shrewd as snakes and as innocent as doves." About this passage Martin Luther King, Jr. notes the apparent paradox between the shrewdness of a snake and the innocence of a dove. He points out that this dissonance is precisely what Jesus intends: "We must combine the toughness of the serpent and the softness of the dove, a tough mind and a tender heart."[9] What characterizes a tough mind is:

> incisive thinking, realistic appraisal, and decisive judgment. The tough mind is sharp and penetrating, breaking through the crust of legends and myths and shifting the true from the false. The tough minded individual is astute and discerning. He [sic] has a strong, austere quality that makes for firmness of purpose and solidness of commitment.[10]

Tough-minded people are thoughtful. When we looked at the philosophy of Hannah Arendt earlier in the book, we saw that at the heart of banal evil is the danger of thoughtlessness, the inability to think beyond the parameters of what you assume you already know, combined with a lack of empathy, compassion, critical thinking, or concern. Thoughtless people don't bother to ask questions, and when they do, they ask the wrong ones. When a government says, "Yes, of course we will deal with the problem of Christian persecution" and then does nothing, thoughtless people say: "Ah well, I'm sure they will sort it out," and never raise the issue again. Thoughtless people are greedy, covetous, and self-centred, hoarding goods and love (just in case we might need it). Thoughtless people will simply click their mouses and think nothing of the consequences. Thoughtless people fail to challenge their churches

9. King, *A Gift of Love*, 2.

10. King, *A Gift of Love*, 2.

when the politics of nationalism rather than their identity in Jesus threatens to form their identity.

Tough minded people take seriously Paul's call for our minds to be renewed. In order that they can see through illusions and test and approve what God's will is—"his good, pleasing, and perfect will" (Rom 12:2). In a world in which powerful forces try to persuade us that there is no such thing as truth, and that only their version of the world is worthy of respect, tough-mindedness and critical thinking are vital skills that we need to learn and to teach our children.

But tough-mindedness and critical thinking on their own are not the only things that we need as we participate in the war of the lamb. We also need gentleness and tenderness. As King puts it:

> Toughmindedness without tenderheartedness is cold and detached, leaving one's life in a perpetual winter devoid of the warmth of spring and the gentle heat of summer. . . . The hardhearted person never truly loves. He engages in a crass utilitarianism which values other people mainly according to their usefulness to him. He never experiences the beauty of friendship, because he is too cold to feel affection for another and is too self-centred to share another's joy and sorrow. He is an isolated island. No outpouring of love links him with the mainland of humanity.[11]

Even when we are challenged, we are called to remember gentleness: "Opponents must be gently instructed, in the hope that God will grant them repentance leading them to a knowledge of the truth" (2 Tim 2:25). "God has two outstretched arms. One is strong enough to surround us with justice, and one is gentle enough to embrace us with love. . . . I am thankful that we worship a God who is both toughminded and tenderhearted."[12] Spiritual warfare requires that we act with the tough-mindedness and tender-heartedness of God's love.

11. King, *A Gift of Love*, 5.
12. King, *A Gift of Love*, 8.

Love and worship

A central aspect of the Lamb's war is the practice of worship. Worship is the place where we learn to be oriented towards love and goodness. Worship is the place where we are formed to be tough-minded and tender-hearted. Worship is the place where we acknowledge our helplessness and need of God's deliverance, and in so doing learn how to move to God's rhythm of redemption.

In concluding this book, there are three aspects of worship that it will be helpful to place alongside of the other modes of resistance to evil that we have looked at thus far.

Eucharist, Christian Identity, and Resistance to Evil

Earlier in the book I emphasized the importance of Christian identity for the formation of people who can effectively resist evil. As we have seen, claiming Christian identity does not necessarily help us to avoid evil. The Rwandan genocide sharply and powerfully brought to the fore the danger of allowing one's cultural identity to take priority over one's Christian identity. This phenomenon is not unique to Rwanda. It is a temptation for all of us. This temptation is revealed in concentrated form in the rise of the extreme right in the United States and Europe. Here Christian identity is an integral part of evil thinking and action.

The dangers of Christian identity: The radical right

White supremacy organisations such as "Christian Identity," "Soldiers of Odin," and "Phineas Priests[13]" regard themselves as holy warriors and find their inspiration in religious concepts and Scriptural interpretations. Central to the ideology of such groups is hatred of other faiths, such as Judaism or Islam, and violent

13. For an interesting critical exploration of these groups see Southern Poverty Law Center, "Holy Hate: The Far Right's Radicalization of Religion."

acts carried out and justified in the name of Christianity. While arguably small in number, they are nonetheless influential. One example is the organization Christian Identity:

> With its ideology linked to numerous domestic terrorist attacks in the late 20th century, . . . [Christian Identity] has significantly influenced the development of American far-right extremism. As an antisemitic and racist belief system, Christian Identity provides religious justification for violence and domestic terrorism. Although the traditional CI movement has declined, Christian Identity has risen in importance as a radicalizing and mobilizing force within existing neofascist accelerationist communities.[14]

With the widespread use of social media and its ability to influence large numbers of people, it makes little difference how many people are formally involved with an organization such as this. A small number of people can influence and radicalize individuals and groups not only in their local vicinity but across the world. Central to the tactics of such organization is random and intentionally destabilizing violence. Adherents assume they are engaged in a racial holy war within which violence is assumed to be beneficial:

> Instigating violence can be seen as acting as God's soldier or acting out God's will. Additionally, in accelerationist groups that are already prone to violence, Christian Identity can be used as a religious justification for acts they already want to commit. Christian Identity ideology also gives extremists religious backing for their antisemitic and racist beliefs by merging racism and antisemitism with religion.[15]

Such Christian-inspired violence is not confined to the United States. On the 22 July 2011 Anders Breivik planted a bomb under the Government office buildings in Oslo, Norway, killing eight

14. Middlebury Institute of International Studies at Monterey, "Christian Identity's New Role in the Extreme Right."

15. Middlebury Institute, "Christian Identity's New Role in the Extreme Right."

people with many more injured. He then headed to the Island of Utøya where he killed seventy-seven young people who were there for a retreat of the Norwegian Labour Party's youth organization, wounding many more. Islamic terrorism was assumed to be the motivation for the attack:

> Amidst the fallout from the event, the wide-spread assumption voiced by the media and broadcast worldwide over the internet, radio, and television was that the perpetrator of these attacks was a Muslim terrorist, and, it was implied, not an ethnic Norwegian. The general consensus was that very few would have expected the terrorist to be a Caucasian Norwegian, born and raised in the affluent west end area of Oslo—as he was later revealed to be. Furthermore, it was highly unexpected when it transpired that the terrorist associated his violent acts with Christianity, using biblical texts to encourage and try to justify "warfare" against Muslims and multiculturalism. . . . [T]he very idea of "Christian," "biblically" inspired terrorism in Europe was seemingly so unthinkable that it has not been given any serious attention: indeed, once it became clear that the perpetrator was not Muslim, attention to his religious affiliation has vanished from view.[16]

It is interesting that the religious dimension of this horrible act faded into the background when it was discovered Breivik was Christian rather than Muslim. His actions didn't seem to meet the cultural expectation of religious terrorism or who carries it out. But the Bible seems to have been at the heart of Breivik's thinking. Hannah Strømmen points out that for Breivik the "Bible functions as a legitimating device for terror, glossing violence as defence of a Christian God and a Christian Europe; as a motivational instrument, positing God as a fellow fighter; and, finally, as a point of origin for a Christian, mono-cultural Europe."[17]

Breivik's Christian identity was quite specifically cultural rather than focused on institutional religion. He saw Christianity as a cultural, social identity and a moral platform that underpinned

16. Strømmen, "Christian Terror in Europe?," 148.

17. Strømmen "Christian Terror in Europe?," 148.

his thought and actions.[18] He believed in a kind of Christianity that did not necessarily require God or a commitment to Jesus. Christian identity had to do with pledging allegiance to a cultural moral system that was underpinned by Christian beliefs and within which violence and racial supremacy was an assumed the correct Christian way to behave.[19]

It would be easy simply to dismiss Breivik and the other groups we have touched on here, as "not *really* Christian." There would be truth in that. It is difficult to see how the lovers of a God who *is* love can relish violence and separation. However, to do that is to open ourselves to the temptation to make the issues primarily moral, political, and legal rather than theological. Distorted Christian identity needs to be countered by the truth of the gospel. When people claim to be doing evil in the name of God, we need to ask the question "Is it true?"

Holy hatred?

We do not have space here to explore all of the complex dynamics of the kind of distorted Christian identity that lies behind Christian violence and terrorism. We can however push into the central dynamic that fuels the theology and the practice of these kinds of movements: *hatred.* Roughly defined:

> Hatred is an intense negative emotional response towards certain people, things, or ideas, usually related to opposition or revulsion toward something. . . . Hatred

18. Strømmen "Christian Terror in Europe?," 152.

19. This may be why Brenton Tarrant who murdered forty-nine people and injured many more in the 2019 Christchurch killings in New Zealand was ambiguous about his Christian connections. As he put it: "It is complicated. When I know, I will tell you." Tarrant was a follower of Breivik and indeed wrote to him to ask for his "blessing" before carrying out the attack. It may be that the complication relates to Breivik's idea that one can be a cultural Christian without believing in God. Breivik wrote that his followers "don't need to have a personal relationship with God or Jesus to fight for our Christian cultural heritage. It is enough that you are a Christian-agnostic or a Christian atheist." Watts, "Breivik's Christ-less 'Christianity.'"

> is often associated with intense feelings of anger, contempt, and disgust. Hatred is sometimes seen as the opposite of love.[20]

The suggestion that hatred is the opposite of love should immediately raise a red flag for any Christians who find themselves using the language of hatred. Worshipping a God who *is* love (1 John 4:8) while at the same time hating other human beings is a manifestation of the kind of evil we have been exploring throughout this book. Nevertheless, one might ask: "but does the Bible not talk about holy hatred: a form of hatred that somehow mirrors the hatred of God and is justifiable in the face of evil?" It is the case that there are passages of Scripture that do seem to justify hatred and violence. For example, on Psalm 139:21–22 we find the psalmist apparently urging us to hate our enemies:

> Do I not hate those who hate you, Lord,
> and abhor those who are in rebellion against you?
> I have nothing but hatred for them;
> I count them my enemies.

It is not difficult to see how someone whose Christian identity has become misshapen in the ways we have described above might draw upon a passage like this to justify violence in the name of God. However, if we look at this passage in the light of Scripture as a whole, there seems to be a clear contradiction between the love and forgiveness of enemies that Jesus proclaims under the new covenant (Matt 5:43–48), and the idea apparently expressed here, that hatred and violence are God's way of resolving conflict. How can such a tension be resolved? How can "perfect hate" be understood as a mode of perfect love?

Hating the right things

Hating something is not necessarily wrong. I hate seeing people who are suffering. In the light of our definition of hatred, this does

20. Wikipedia, "Hatred" (accessed on 18 August 2022).

not seem inappropriate. My hatred manifests my lack of love for seeing people suffer. The apostle Paul hates doing the things that he doesn't want to do but can't seem to help himself from doing them: "Sometimes I do not understand why I yield to the things I do. There are things I know I should be doing, yet I am not. And I find myself doing things that I actually hate . . . wretched man that I am, who shall deliver me from this body of death" (Rom 7:15, 24). Paul has no love for the ungodly things that he does, so hatred seems to be an appropriate term to use. Likewise, our definition of evil would indicate that God hates oppression and injustice.[21] However, the *context* and the *goal* of such hatred is key. If God is love (context), then hatred has a goal: *to overcome hatred with love.*[22] God's hatred (and that of those who claim to follow God) is not something that can be understood apart from God's character: "You have loved righteousness, and hated iniquity. Therefore God, your God, has anointed you with the oil of gladness above your fellows" (Heb 1:9, quoting Ps 45:6–7).

We are to hate evil, whilst at the same time revealing love and mercy to the perpetrators of evil.

Loving your enemies

"You have heard that it was said, 'You shall love your neighbor and hate your enemy.' But I say to you: love your enemies, and pray for those who persecute you" (Matt 5:43–44). If we turn to the teachings of Jesus, we can begin to see how this works itself out in terms of Christian identity. Jesus calls on us to love our enemies and to pray for those who persecute and stand in opposition to us. It is not that we are to ignore sinfulness or those things that stand

21. I recognise the danger of anthropomorphising God here. God does not have emotions in the way that human beings do, because God is not simply a human being writ large. Nonetheless, when it comes to thinking about how God hates injustice, the term "hate" still holds relevance in making the point that God is against everything that stands against God's love.

22. "Do not be overcome by evil, but overcome evil with good" (Rom 12:21).

against God. It is the manner in which we are to stand against evil that reveals the authenticity of our Christian identity. As Paul puts it, "Do not be overcome by evil, but overcome evil with good" (Rom 12:21). We are called to love our enemies for what and whom they are: people made in the image of a God who *is* love. This is our beginning point for hating the evil that people do. As we learn to love our neighbors for what they are, so we begin to hate those things that block us from the love of God and distract us into worshiping things that are lesser than God, be that money, work, violence, injustice, or whatever. *It is this kind of hatred that drives Christian into radical acts of love.*

In the light of the teachings of Jesus, the "perfect hate" that the psalmist talks about should not manifest itself in violence and the depersonalization of our enemies. "Perfect hate" is an aspect of faithfully loving our neighbor as ourselves and working towards overcoming those things that prevent *all of us together* from flourishing in our friendship with God, self, and one another. This is the counter that reflects Jesus's first response to the extreme violence of the cross: "Father forgive them."

Speaking out: holding on to Christian identity

With these thoughts in mind, we can begin to see some basic principles that can lovingly reveal and push against toxic Christian identities in all of the various forms that they take:

1. *All human beings are made in the image of* God (Gen 1:27). We are therefore called to be with people who share our faith and those who do not, and to learn to live peaceably with those with whom we agree and those with whom we disagree. That is not to suggest that we need to agree with everyone or always be seeking compromise and the middle ground. It *is* to point out that *the ways in which we disagree matter*. Learning to live well with those who see things differently (inside and outside of the church) is crucial for the envisioning and living out of the gospel.

2. *Hatred, arrogance, judgmentalism, lack of humility, and violence are the antithesis of Christian love.* The fact that we might act in these ways and assume that we are right and that this is what God *really* wants indicates the presence of evil. "Love is patient, love is kind. It does not envy, it does not boast, it is not proud. It does not dishonor others, it is not self-seeking, it is not easily angered, it keeps no record of wrongs" (1 Cor 13:4–5). Hatred of the wrong things is a mode of evil. Hatred of the right things can be a blessing. We must learn how *to hate with love.*

3. *Hospitality and the love of one's neighbor is central to Christian identity. We are called to build relationships across creedal, racial, sexual, and national boundaries* (John 4:1–42; Luke 10:25--37; Gal 3:28). The neighbors whom we are called to love will often be those whom we assume to be "outsiders" (Luke 10:25–37). Hospitality is a practice of love that teaches us to hate the right things.

4. *When Christianity is misrepresented by any given individual or group it is the responsibility of Christian communities to speak the truth in love* (Eph 4:15). Silence, ambiguity, and inaction are modes of evil.[23]

Eucharist, Christian identity, and radical inclusion

All of this leads us to the first of our spiritual practices that will help deliver us from evil: the *Eucharist*. Sitting at the heart of the worshiping community is the sacrament of the Eucharist (or Holy Communion, the Mass, the Lord's Supper, depending on your tradition). The Eucharist is the place where we learn peace, discover how to love, and are taught what to hate. As we eat the bread and drink the wine, we remember who Jesus was, what he said, and what he did. In the brokenness of the elements, we

23. For an interesting exploration of the dangers of ambiguity in the face of right-wing violence, see Townsend, "The Day No One Would Say the Nazis Were Bad."

discover the brokenness of the body of Jesus and the redemptive disruptive power of his blood, which was spilled for our redemption. In the brokenness of Jesus, we discover the brokenness of humanity and the source of our healing.

The Eucharist is a symbol of the new covenant given by God through the life, death, and resurrection of Jesus. The old covenant was given to Israel by God when God freed them from slavery. The new covenant represents the freeing of human beings from the bondage of sin. The Eucharist is a sacrament, an enacted truth, a visible sign of an invisible grace. As we participate in the sacrament, as we remember Jesus, we are enabled to see the world through sacramental eyes that allow us to view creation in the light of what God has done in the death and resurrection of Jesus. The Eucharist is therefore:

1. *a place of reconciliation, incorporation, and peace*: peace with God, peace with others, peace with oneself, given through the sacrifice of Jesus;
2. *a place of fellowship and love where we discover that we are tied together in the Spirit by God, to God, and for God.* As we realize this, we discover that we are bound to one another with bonds of sacrificial love. The ritual reminds us that our citizenship is simultaneously of this world and the world to come (Phil 3:20), and that the love that we will experience in all of its fullness in the future can be felt, touched, and seen—even if only through a glass darkly—in the present (1 Cor 13:12). It gives us peace "until he comes" (1 Cor 11:26);
3. *a place of critique and discernment.* The Eucharist is a place where we are questioned about our identity as Christians. Do we belong to the world with all of its ambiguities and brokenness, or do we belong to Jesus and the new life that he promises? We are challenged as to whom and how we should follow. Do we choose to follow the ways of society, or do we choose to follow Jesus? The Eucharist reminds us that Jesus's radical way of love is life in all of its fullness.

By constantly reminding us of the way of Jesus, over time the Eucharist forms our identity into the shape of Jesus. In turn, it sends us back out into the world to be emissaries of Jesus's Eucharistic love. *The Eucharist is a practice that forms us as people who are capable of resisting evil.*

When is the Eucharist not the Eucharist and why does it matter?

We should not however be triumphalistic about the Eucharist. It is central to Christian identity and the avoidance of the kinds of evil we have highlighted in this book. But it is also open to distortion, as Paul discovered in the church at Corinth. There were clearly divisions within the Corinthian church with regard to the Eucharist. The problem seems to have been that the rich and powerful were eating and drinking to excess during the Eucharistic meal, and the poorer and less powerful within the congregation were left with nothing:

> In the following directives I have no praise for you, for your meetings do more harm than good. In the first place, I hear that when you come together as a church, there are divisions among you, and to some extent I believe it. No doubt there have to be differences among you to show which of you have God's approval. So then, when you come together, it is not the Lord's Supper you eat, for when you are eating, some of you go ahead with your own private suppers. As a result, one person remains hungry and another gets drunk. Don't you have homes to eat and drink in? Or do you despise the church of God by humiliating those who have nothing? What shall I say to you? Shall I praise you? Certainly not in this matter! (1 Cor 11:17–22)

Paul's concern is not simply a matter of fairness. His concern is with the faithfulness of the Corinthians and whether or not they were actually doing what they were claiming to do. In verse 20 Paul makes a rather enigmatic comment: "So then, when you come together, it is not the Lord's Supper you eat, for when you are eating, some of you go ahead with your own private suppers." What could Paul mean by this? Clearly the Corinthians were eating and drinking and assuming they were participating in the Lord's Supper. But how could they be participating in the Lord's Supper and at the same time *not* participating in it? Theologian Julie Land recognizes this dissonance and points to the importance of the Greek term *synerchesthai* ("come together"). This term, which is used

> at the beginning of this unit, 11:17, and repeated in 11:18, 20, 33, and 34, pinpoints the problem Paul is addressing in the Corinthians' practice of gathering for worship. *Synerchesthai* can denote "to assemble for a meeting," or, "to be united," and according to Richard Hays, "Paul's rebuke to the Corinthians plays off of this double sense of the term: when they 'come together' as a church they paradoxically do not 'come together' in unity and peace.[24]

The Corinthians *think/assume* they are coming together and participating in the Lord's Supper, but Paul indicates that something quite different is happening. The Corinthians are indeed coming together, but not in the way that God intends eucharistic *synerchesthai*/coming together to be. Land points out that it is not the *intention* of the Corinthians that makes the ritual authentic. It is the living out of the meaning of the practice that counts. (Remember our previous observation that it is not necessarily the *intentions* of actions that make them evil but the *outcome*):

> The Corinthians are gathering in a sociological sense for the common meal, yet it is not the Lord's Supper (11:20). With this reading (of 11:20) it seems a eucharistic gathering is not dependent on one's right psychological intentions, however, nor does it seem that perfectly performed ritual overrides the relationship between those gathered (11:20–22). The way in which those who gather together

24. Land, "Remember as Re-membering," 154. Quoting Hays, *First Corinthians*, 194.

> for worship relate to one another appears importantly significant (11:20–22).[25]

Some are eating and drinking to excess, others not at all. Importantly, in 11:21, Paul uses the term *idiom deipnon* ("one's own meal"). Land points out that within the apostolic tradition "key texts depict *idion* and *koinon* as explicitly in contrast to one another. Consequently, Paul asserts, this meal they are eating, it is their own private meal; it is not the Lord's Supper (11:20–21). And it is not the Lord's Supper because they do not eat, but because they are not truly together when they eat."[26] As Richard Hays puts it: "the meal that should be the symbol and seal of their oneness has in fact become an occasion for some of them to shame others (11:21–22).[27] The ritual of Communion—being together in a context where there are no divisions between rich and poor, male and female, strong and weak—demands that the practice it represents is lived out. If the Corinthians practice did not match the intention of the ritual, they were not truly engaging in the ritual even if it looked as though they were. *Simply engaging in the ritual does not make the ritual what it claims to be.* It is only when the ritual is lived out within the church and from there on into society that it truly becomes the Lord's Supper. The problem seems to have been that the practice of the Eucharist was reflecting the assumptions of society rather than the radical assumptions of a different kingdom with a radically different king.

Living into our eucharistic identity

The observation that the Corinthians were taking their guide from society rather than from the intention of the ritual is important. It is certainly the case that the Eucharist is a place where our identity is reinforced, and all of the blessings outlined previously (should) become embodied in God's people. However, the

25. Land, "Remember as Re-membering," 155.
26. Land, "Remember as Re-membering," 155.
27. Hays, *First Corinthians*, 193.

intention of the Eucharist is not to ensure conformity to the ritual, but rather to allow the ritual to conform people to the ways of God. It calls people to examine themselves, but not only in terms of their personal morality (although it does do this), but also to their corporate responsibility, particularly to the poor, the vulnerable, and the outcast. The Corinthians were ignoring the poor. In conforming to the social expectations of the day, they failed to do anything other than have a series of personal meals which they fooled themselves into thinking was the Lord's Supper.

We were rightly shocked earlier in this book when we highlighted the fact that Rwandan Christians left church and went off to participate in the genocide. The question raised by Paul's concerns about the Corinthian church give us pause to reflect on whether or not a similar dynamic may not be at work within our own lives. Paul's rebuke of the Corinthian church speaks into such questions and demands that we remember the *actions* that the Eucharist is intended to produce as well as the inherent meaning that it is intended to teach us. Do we leave the Eucharist with a passion to defend the poor and fight against injustice? What happens if we take the sacrament and continue to hate the people that we hated before we ate and drank? Are we really taking the Lord's Supper, or are we eating our own meal? Who is missing from the Eucharistic table?[28] What happens if we take the sacrament and continue to

28. Land points out how this resonates with the ways in which some people with intellectual disabilities are prevented from participating in the sacrament because it is assumed they do not have the level of knowledge necessary to ensure the sacrament is efficacious. This raises a number of questions. How much knowledge of Jesus is enough and who says where the barrier sits? Why do we assume that intellectual affirmation of written and verbal formulations of faith are the "true" way to come to know God? Do we come to know God through our intellect or through the whole of our bodies? I have written on these kinds of questions elsewhere (*Becoming Friends of Time*). Here I simply want to point out that within Western culture intellect and reason are prized as crucial dimensions of our humanness, so much so that if we lose them or never have such capacities, some would see this as grounds either to prevent our birth or to hasten our death (e.g., Singer, *Practical Ethics*). Questions around the level of intellect that a person needs to participate in the Eucharist do not emerge from the inclusive, loving dynamic that we encounter in Scripture wherein the weak, the poor, and the downtrodden are prioritised. Rather, they

live lives that are unforgiving, fractious, and unaccepting of difference? What happens if we take the sacrament and then remain silent about the evil that surrounds us, "sure" and "safe" in our own personal reconciliation with God? We need to be very careful that we understand what it means to live eucharistic lives that truly reflect the meaning of the ritual. There is nothing wrong with having a good meal on your own, but if Jesus is eating elsewhere.

Living the Psalms: Lamentation and Imprecation as Modes of Resistance

The act of worship is complex. On the one hand, worship is a tender-hearted affair in which we pour out our hearts to God in praise. We sing, raise our hands, and worship the King of kings. Worship is a time of great celebration for the good things that God has done and will do in the future.

At the center of the Bible sits the Book of Psalms, what Bonhoeffer called "the prayer book of the Bible."[29] Here we discover both the tough-mindedness and the tender-heartedness of God.

The royal psalms capture something of this celebration of the faithfulness of God and the deep desire to live safely in God's emerging kingdom (Pss 2, 18, 20, 21, 45, 72, 101, 110, 132, 144):

> I love you, LORD, my strength.
>
> The LORD is my rock, my fortress and my deliverer;
> my God is my rock, in whom I take refuge,

are a reflection of an assumption that a) we are individual selves who, through our intellect and reason, make our own decisions, and b) that God's love can be communicated conceptually without taking cognisance of the fact that God may communicate God's love in a multitude of different ways which may or may not prioritise the intellect. When people with intellectual disabilities are excluded from the eucharistic table we are engaging in a similar clouding of the boundaries between the values of the church and the values of society that Paul encountered in the Corinthian church. For a further development of this point, see Stiff, "Keeping the Feast."

29. Bonhoeffer, *Psalms: The Prayer Book of the Bible.*

my shield and the horn of my salvation, my stronghold.

I called to the LORD, who is worthy of praise,
and I have been saved from my enemies. (Ps 18:1–3)

Here we hear the call of victory and the assurance of hope. Other psalms speak quite beautifully about the gentleness and protective love of God:

He will cover you with his feathers,
and under his wings you will find refuge;
his faithfulness will be your shield and rampart. (Ps 91:4)

God's love is deeply tender-hearted.

The language of suffering

On the other hand, the psalms remind us that worship is also a tough-minded business, which draws our attention to evil, injustice, frustration, abandonment, God's apparent inaction, and sometimes even violence and retribution. These psalms (e.g., 13, 44, 60, 74, 79) take very seriously suffering and injustice:

You have rejected us, God, and burst upon us;
you have been angry—now restore us!
You have shaken the land and torn it open;
mend its fractures, for it is quaking.
You have shown your people desperate times;
you have given us wine that makes us stagger.
But for those who fear you, you have raised a banner
to be unfurled against the bow.

Save us and help us with your right hand,
that those you love may be delivered. (Ps 60: 1–5)

It is no coincidence that there are more psalms of lament than any other kind of psalm. God has given us a language to speak out our outrage at the power of evil and its effect on human beings. The psalms of lament teach us that profound sadness, suffering, grief, and righteous anger towards evil are real and need to be articulated. However, that articulation always happens in the presence of God. The psalms of lament are not a cry into the void. They are articulations of grief, sadness, confusion, and anger that are spoken (and sometimes shouted) to God. Evil is *awful*. But we are never alone in our sadness and brokenness, even though it sometimes feels like the opposite is the case, as the writer of Psalm 88 makes quite clear sometimes: "Darkness is my only companion . . . ." Lament is important because it is profoundly honest and at points quite dreadful. At the same time, it is sometimes overwhelmingly hopeful. The biblical scholar Ellen Davis puts it this way:

> When you lament in good faith, opening yourself to God honestly and fully—no matter what you have to say—then you are beginning to clear the way for praise. You are straining toward the time when God will turn your tears into laughter. When you lament, you are asking God to create the conditions in which it will become possible for you to offer praise—conditions, it turns out, that are mainly within your own heart.[30]

Most of the psalms of lament have a particular structure.[31] Psalm 13 is a helpful example.

> How long, LORD? Will you forget me forever?
> How long will you hide your face from me?
>
> How long must I wrestle with my thoughts
> and day after day have sorrow in my heart?
> How long will my enemy triumph over me?

30. Davis, *Getting Involved with God*, 15.

31. In a previous book, *Raging with Compassion*, I spent a considerable amount of time looking at the lament psalms. I argued that they were a good example of practical theodicy, that is, a practical way of dealing with evil that doesn't try to explain the presence of evil. Instead, these psalms recognize and articulate the fullness and reality of evil, but always within the context of prayer. I won't repeat the arguments I made there, but noting a couple of key points will be helpful.

Look on me and answer, LORD my God.
Give light to my eyes, or I will sleep in death,

and my enemy will say, "I have overcome him,"
and my foes will rejoice when I fall.

But I trust in your unfailing love;
  my heart rejoices in your salvation.

I will sing the LORD's praise,
  for he has been good to me.

This psalm begins with a deep-rooted expression of pain, lostness, alienation, and disappointment at God's absence and lack of action. "How long LORD will you forget me forever?" (Ps 13:1). Evil seems to be winning. But then having spoken out his pain, the psalmist makes an important turn (vv. 5 and 6). Something changes. The horrible situation that he is addressing remains the same but suddenly, for whatever reason, the psalmist remembers God's unfailing love. Doing so reframes the entire situation. The evil remains, but praise, love, and redemption have now become a possibility, even in the midst of disaster. God will deal with delivering us fully from the evil in the long run. For now, the psalmist has discovered God's unfailing love, and this allows him to move from lamentation to praise.

In this way the psalms of lament help us to resist the hopelessness that accompanies evil by providing a faith-filled language to articulate our pain, disappointment, loss, and fear, always in the presence of God. The psalms of lament allow our worship practices to be a place where we learn to be a people of lament. In this way we are enabled to break out of the fear and isolation that is an inevitable companion of the presence of evil. Lament shapes and forms us in the ways of hope, love, and tough-mindedness and tender-heartedness. In many ways this pattern of lament runs all the way through this book. My hope for you, my readers, is that the resolve "But I trust in your unfailing love" will become your goal even amidst the most difficult of times.

The psalms of imprecation

Lamentation is thus a useful ally in our fight with evil. But there is another form of psalm that we might find helpful, one that is often overlooked or avoided, but which has a good deal to offer: *the psalms of imprecation* or of cursing. At first glance we might assume that these cursing psalms could never be places where we learn how to love God, neighbor, and enemy. But a closer look reveals something interesting.

The psalms of imprecation are not just tough minded: they are downright disturbing! When the psalmist cries out: "Happy is the one who seizes your infants and dashes them against the rocks" (Ps 137:9), there is not much room for tender-heartedness! And yet such imprecatory psalms are part of the psalter, part of God's word to us, part of the prayer book of the Bible, and as such, part of our worship. How might we faithfully use them as an aspect of our spiritual warfare?

i. The body of Christ is broken

Old Testament scholar Ellen Davis offers us an interesting way into this issue. She begins by noting that often the psalms of imprecation "reckon directly with a feature of church life which is almost never acknowledged: the phenomenon of *betrayal within the faith community*."[32] For example, in Psalm 55:13–15 the psalmist informs us that

> It is not an enemy who reviles me; that I could bear. It is not my opponent who vaunts himself against me; I could hide from him. But you, someone just like me, my companion and my intimate; we shared sweet fellowship in the house of God, we walked in the crowd.[33]

All of us who have spent time within Christian communities will have experienced the beauty of loving community and

32. Davis, *Getting Involved with God*, 25.

33. Davis, *Getting Involved with God*, 25.

the tragedy of broken relationships. "The cursing psalms help us to hold our anger in good faith."[34] They give us a language, sharp as it may be, to talk about betrayal inside the body of Christ, as well as evils that come from elsewhere. They cannot be the final word about our enemies, but they clearly articulate something of the ways in which we do, on occasion, feel towards even our brothers and sisters in Christ, and indeed towards a whole array of other people. Honest expression of such feelings helps prevent them from fermenting into evil. Healing comes through articulating the wound, not by covering it up or pretending it is not there. False piety only brings on anxiety, depression, and loathing of self and others. We would love to love our enemies in the way Jesus commands us to, but even to begin to try to do that we need to clear some ground and express our anger. Acknowledging our rage without yielding to it opens a space for healing. As Davis puts it: "we must offer them [i.e, our feelings of fury], along with our more attractive gifts, for God's work of transformation."[35] The imprecatory psalms thus provide us with a language to express not just our anger but our rage.

Second, and importantly in relation to God's ultimate victory over evil,

> because these psalms come to us as divinely given "counselors," we can trust their teaching that vengeful anger is one mode of access to God. "O God of my praise" (109:1), the psalmist begins. The cry for vengeance is not self-expression but prayer, based on what we know to be true: God is manifest in judgment as well as in mercy. The God who created us for life together (Genesis 2:18) is, like us, outraged by those who violate trust and rupture community. The cursing psalms obliquely affirm that every believer has a share in the prophetic task of naming and renouncing evil, including evil within the community of faith, including evil that is directed against ourselves. There is nothing pre-Christian about that.[36]

34. Davis, *Getting Involved with God*, 25.
35. Davis, *Getting Involved with God*, 25–26.
36. Davis, *Getting Involved with God*, 26–27.

It is of course important to note the direction of these psalms: they are requests for *God* to act:

> the cry for vengeance invariably takes the form of an appeal for God to act. Help me, O LORD my God; deliver me according to your covenant loyalty that they may know that this hand of yours—you yourself, O LORD, have done it (109:26–27). No personal vendetta is authorized, no pouring sugar in the gas tank, no picking up a gun or hiring one. On the contrary, the validity of any punishing action that may occur depends entirely on its being God's action, not ours.[37]

Whether God does in fact act in these ways is not the point. The vengeful request is *offered to God* and then it is *left with God* to deal with. Put slightly differently, these psalms urge us not to engage directly with the powers that bring about violence, vengeance, and revenge, but instead to hand over even our darkest thoughts to the God of justice and love. When we do this, we begin to overcome evil with good, even if our words are sometimes harsh and difficult.

But there is more.

ii. What happens when we are not angry?

There is one last dimension of the psalms of imprecation upon which it is valuable to reflect in the light of our thinking about evil. *What role might these psalms play when we are not angry or vengeful?* Reflecting on this question draws us to perhaps the most challenging aspect of the imprecatory psalms. What if *we* are the enemy against whom the psalmist is railing? Davis urges us to turn the psalms a full 180 degrees until they are directed at ourselves, until we ask, "Is there anyone in the community of God's people who might want to say this to God about me—or maybe, about us?"[38] Take, for example, Psalm 10:1–3.

> Why, O Lord, do you stand far away?

37. Davis, *Getting Involved with God*, 27.

38. Davis, *Getting Involved with God*, 28.

Why do you hide yourself in times of trouble?
In arrogance the wicked hotly pursue the poor.
let them be caught in the schemes that they have devised.
For the wicked boasts of the desires of his soul,
and the one greedy for gain curses and renounces the LORD.

Think about that statement in relation to the idea of the scarcity mentality that we discussed in chapter 2. Could the psalmist be talking about *us*? Could *we* be the ones who hide in a time of trouble? Could *we* be the ones who hotly pursue the poor? Or take Psalm 109:16, 21–22:

> Let [her] memory be cut off from the earth, because [she] did not remember to act in covenant faith but hounded a person poor and needy, crushed in heart, even to death. . . . But you, O LORD, act with me as befits your Name. Because your covenant faithfulness is good, deliver me. For I am poor and needy, and my heart is pierced within me.[39]

Who could legitimately say this of *us*? Who could say that we or you hounded a poor and needy person, or one who was crushed in heart? Who could say that we or you did not remember in covenant faith? Could it be the mother whose child has just died from malnutrition when there is more than enough food in the world to go around? Could the individuals and families that lie behind the statistics in the introduction to this book speak of you in this way? Could it be the persecuted Christians to whom we pay little or no attention? Could it be the women and men who are trapped in the crushing wheels of pornography, damaged, broken, and sometimes destroyed by a myriad of tiny mouse clicks? Could it be the countries whose history has been marked by our country's colonialism and who now live in poverty and lostness because of circumstances of geography and history that are not of their own making? If the psalmist is right that "good will come to those who are generous and lend freely, who conduct their affairs with

39. Davis, *Getting Involved with God*, 28–29.

justice" (Ps 112:5), then what will happen to those of us who refuse to be generous and who ignore justice? Certainly, we could claim that we didn't know. But will that be a legitimate excuse when the day comes for us to face the Lord?

The psalms of imprecation draw attention to the fact that when Jesus tells us to love our enemies, it is *we* who might be the enemy others are called to love. When Jesus tells the parable of the wheat and the tares, and informs us that "an enemy did this," it may be that *we* are that enemy. What if we are in fact unconscious tares rather than flourishing wheat, the propagators of evil rather than the bringers of love. This kind of honest, tough-minded, and self-reflective worship helps remove us from forms of idolatry that "reduce God to an extension of our own embattled and wounded egos."[40] They help us to see where our allegiances lie and what really forms our identities. The cursing psalms may be raw, difficult, and dissonant, but they may also be absolutely necessary for developing the kind of renewed minds and honest, solid Christian identity that will lead us out of temptation and help us to recognize the need for God's deliverance.

Conclusion

With this we conclude our all too brief foray into evil. We have seen how all of us in various ways can easily get caught up in the processes of evil. If we are not alert and aware, evil will crash in on us, sometimes in silence and at other points like a roaring lion. We have explored how things like trust, generosity, friendship, justice, prayer, worship, Eucharist, lamentation, and imprecation help to shape and form us into people who can see and resist temptation and be open to God's deliverance from evil. Paul tells us: "Do not be overcome by evil but overcome evil with good." Ultimately the victory has been won through the cross and resurrection of Jesus. But for now, it is our Christian responsibility to resist evil and to

40. Davis, *Getting Involved with God*, 26.

do good. I pray that this book has provided some tools for that journey. These days are dark and difficult. These days will pass. God will deliver us.

Bibliography

Ames, Paul. “Two Rwandan Nuns Convicted of War Crimes.” *ABC News*, June 8, 2001. https://abcnews.go.com/International/story?id=80960&page =1#:~:text=Sister%20Gertrude%20Mukangango%20and%20 Sister,burned%20and%20butchered%20to%20death.

“Amnesty International Condemns Rich Countries for Hoarding Covid-19 Vaccines.” Amnesty International, April 7, 2021. https://www.france24.com/en/europe/20210407-amnesty-condemns-rich-countries-for-hoarding-covid-19-vaccines.

Arendt, Hannah. *Eichmann in Jerusalem: A Report on the Banality of Evil*. London: Penguin, 1964.

———. *The Origins of Totalitarianism*. New York: Harcourt Brace, 1951.

Barr, Rachel Anne. “Watching Pornography Rewires the Brain to a More Juvenile State.” *The Conversation*, November 27, 2019. http://theconversation.com/watching-pornography-rewires-the-brain-to-a-more-juvenile-state-127306.

Behr, Rafael. “The Lockdown in Our Minds Will Be the Last Restriction to Be Lifted.” *The Guardian*, April 28, 2020. https://www.theguardian.com/commentisfree/2020/apr/28/lockdown-restrictions-solidarity-coronavirus-social-distancing.

Benhabib, Seyla. *Politics in Dark Times: Encounters with Hannah Arendt*. New York: Cambridge University Press, 2010.

The Bishop of Truro’s Independent Review for the UK Foreign Secretary of Foreign and Commonwealth Office Support for Persecuted Christians. https://christianpersecutionreview.org.uk/.

Bonhoeffer, Dietrich. *Psalms: The Prayer Book of the Bible*. Minneapolis: Fortress, 1974.

Brueggemann, Walter. "The Liturgy of Abundance, The Myth of Scarcity." *The Christian Century*, March 24–31, 1999. https://www.christiancentury.org/article/2012-01/liturgy-abundance-myth-scarcity.

"The Connection between Sex Trafficking and Pornography." Human Trafficking Search, April 14, 2014. https://humantraffickingsearch.org/the-connection-between-sex-trafficking-and-pornography/.

Dallaire, Roméo. *Shake Hands with the Devil: The Failure of Humanity in Rwanda*. Toronto: Random House Canada, 2003.

Davis, Ellen F. *Getting Involved with God: Rediscovering the Old Testament*. Lanham, MD: Cowley, 2001.

Delbanco, Andrew. *The Death of Satan: How Americans Have Lost Their Sense of Evil*. New York: Farrar, Straus, and Giroux, 1995.

Desmond Tutu. Nobel Lecture, December 11, 1984. https://www.nobelprize.org/prizes/peace/1984/tutu/lecture/.

Eastman, Susan. "Empire of Illusion: Sin, Evil, and Good News in Romans." In *Comfortable Words: Essays in Honour of Paul F. M. Zahl*, edited by John D. Koch and Todd H. Brewer, 3–21. Eugene, OR: Pickwick, 2013.

"Florida Man Arrested after Videos of Missing Teen Surface on Pornography Website." *CBS News*, October 25, 2019. https://www.nbcnews.com/news/crime-courts/florida-man-arrested-after-videos-missing-teen-surface-pornography-website-n1072141.

Formosa, P. "Is Radical Evil Banal? Is Banal Evil Radical?" *Philosophy & Social Criticism* 33 (2007) 717–35.

Foster, Richard. "The Peaceable War of the Lamb." *Renovaré,* February 1989. https://renovare.org/articles/the-lambs-war. Accessed August 25, 2021.

Fulford, Ben. "Practices of Compassion and Resistance." Unfinished Theology blog, 2021. https://unfinishedtheology.home.blog/2020/04/07/practices-of-compassion-and-resistance/.

Garbe, L., R. Rau, and T. Toppe. "Influence of Perceived Threat of Covid-19 and HEXACO Personality Traits on Toilet Paper Stockpiling." PLOS ONE 15.6 (2020) e0234232.

Goldhagen, Daniel. *Worse Than War: Genocide, Eliminationism and the Ongoing Assault on Humanity*. New York: Public Affairs, 2009.

Gourevitch, Philip. *We Wish to Inform You That Tomorrow We Will Be Killed with Our Families: Stories from Rwanda* . New York: Picador, 1998.

Hand, Stephen. *Catholic Voices in a World on Fire*. Durham, NC: Lulu.com, 2005.

Hatzfeld, Jean. *Machete Season: The Killers in Rwanda Speak*. New York: Macmillan, 2006.

Hays, Richard B. *First Corinthians*. Interpretation. Louisville, KY: John Knox, 1997.

Hedges, Chris. *The Empire of Illusion: The Loss of Literacy and the Rise of Spectacle*. New York: Nation, 2009.

Holmes, John. "Losing 25,000 to Hunger Every Day." *United Nations Chronicle*. https://www.un.org/en/chronicle/article/losing-25000-hunger-every-day.

"How Many People Are on Porn Sites Right Now?" Fight the New Drug, October 13, 2020. https://fightthenewdrug.org/by-the-numbers-see-how-many-people-are-watching-porn-today/.

Hughes, Dana. "Bill Clinton Regrets Rwanda Now (Not So Much in 1994)." *ABC News*. https://abcnews.go.com/blogs/politics/2014/02/bill-clinton-regrets-rwanda-now-not-so-much-in-1994.

"Human Trafficking by the Numbers." Human Rights First, January 7, 2017. https://www.humanrightsfirst.org/resource/human-trafficking-numbers.

Katongole, Emmanuel. *The Journey of Reconciliation: Groaning for a New Creation in Africa*. Maryknoll, NY: Orbis, 2017. Kindle edition.

Katongole, Emmanuel M., and Jonathan Wilson-Hartgrove. *Mirror to the Church: Resurrecting Faith after Genocide in Rwanda*. Grand Rapids: Zondervan, 2009.

Kelly, Cara. "13 Sex Trafficking Statistics That Explain the Enormity of the Global Sex Trade." *USA Today News*, July 29, 2019. https://eu.usatoday.com/story/news/investigations/2019/07/29/12-trafficking-statistics-enormity-global-sex-trade/1755192001/.

King, Martin Luther. *A Gift of Love: Sermons from Strength to Love and Other Preachings*. Boston: Beacon, 2012.

Kilby, Karen. "Evil and the Limits of Theology." *New Blackfriars* 84.983 (2003) 13–29.

Koch, John D., and Todd H. Brewer, eds. *Comfortable Words: Essays in Honour of Paul F. M. Zahl*. Eugene, OR: Pickwick, 2013.

Koonz, Claudia. *The Nazi Conscience*. Cambridge: Belknap, 2003.

Kristof. Nicholas. "The Children of Pornhub." *New York Times*, December 2020. https://www.nytimes.com/2020/12/04/opinion/sunday/pornhub-rape-trafficking.html.

Land, Julie. "Remember as Re-membering: The Eucharist, 1 Corinthians 11:17–34, and Profound Intellectual Disability." *Studia Liturgica* 50.2 (2020) 152–62.

Livingstone Smith, David. *Less Than Human: Why We Demean, Enslave, and Exterminate Others*. Brighton, UK: Griffin, 2012.

Logue, Jeff. "Pornography Statistics: Who Uses Porn?" October 22, 2015. https://www.sagu.edu/thoughthub/pornography-statistics-who-uses-pornography.

Longman, Timothy. "Christian Churches and Genocide in Rwanda." *Umuvugizi* Revision of paper originally prepared for Conference on Genocide, Religion, and Modernity United States Holocaust Memorial Museum May 11–13, 1997. https://umuvugizi.wordpress.com/2013/04/23/christian-churches-87/.

Mamdani, Muhmood. *When Victims Become Killers: Colonialism, Nativism, and the Genocide in Rwanda*. Princeton, NJ: Princeton University Press, 2001.

McFarland, I. A. "The Problem with Evil." *Theology Today* 74.4 (2018) 321–39.

Middlebury Institute of International Studies at Monterey. "Christian Identity's New Role in the Extreme Right." *Middlebury Institute of International Studies at Monterey*, August 6, 2021. https://www.middlebury.edu/institute/academics/centers-initiatives/ctec/ctec-publications/christian-identitys-new-role-extreme-right.

Neiman, Susan. "Banality Reconsidered." In *Politics in Dark Times: Encounters with Hannah Arendt*, edited by Seyla Benhabib, 305–15. Cambridge: Cambridge University Press, 2010.

"One Million People Sign Petition to Shut Down Pornhub for Alleged Sex Trafficking Videos." *Cision PR Newswire*, June 9, 2020. https://www.prnewswire.com/news-releases/one-million-people-sign-petition-to-shut-down-pornhub-for-alleged-sex-trafficking-videos-301072809.html.

Perry, Samuel. *Addicted to Lust: Pornography in the Lives of Conservative Protestants*. New York: Oxford University Press, 2019.

Pilger, John. "Here Is What Legendary Journalist John Pilger Said about Coronavirus Outbreak." *The Week*, March 12, 2020. https://www.theweek.in/news/world/2020/03/12/here-is-what-legendary-journalist-john-pilger-said-about-coronavirus-outbreak.html.

"Pornhub Removes Millions of Videos after Investigation Finds Child Abuse Content." *The Guardian*, December 14, 2020. https://www.theguardian.com/technology/2020/dec/14/pornhub-purge-removes-unverified-videos-investigation-child-abuse.

"Pornhub under Investigation by Visa, Mastercard amid Abuse Allegations." *Ars Technica*, December 7, 2020. https://arstechnica.com/tech-policy/2020/12/visa-mastercard-investigate-pornhub-amid-allegations-of-child-exploitation.

"Pornography Is Booming during the COVID-19 Lockdowns." *The Economist*, May 10, 2020: https://www.economist.com/international/2020/05/10/pornography-is-booming-during-the-covid-19-lockdowns.

Rai, Tage. "How Could They? Some People Are Ruthless. Some Lose Control. Yet Most Violence Remains Unfathomable. A New Theory Lights Up the Darkness." *Aeon*, June 18, 2015. https://aeon.co/essays/people-resort-to-violence-because-their-moral-codes-demand-it.

———. *Virtuous Violence: Hurting and Killing to Create, Sustain, End, and Honor Social Relationships*. Cambridge: Cambridge University Press, 2014.

Reicher, Stephen, Alex Haslam, and Jay Van Bavel. "How the Stanford Prison Experiment Gave Us the Wrong Idea about Evil." *Prospect*, March 6, 2019. https://www.prospectmagazine.co.uk/magazine/how-the-stanford-prison-experiment-gave-us-the-wrong-ideal-about-evil.

Release International. "Persecution of Christians 'Close to Genocide.'" https://releaseinternational.org/persecution-of-christians-close-to-genocide/.

Rieff, David. "God and Man in Rwanda." *Vanity Fair*, December 1994. https://www.vanityfair.com/magazine/1994/12/rwanda199412.

Ring, Jennifer. "Hannah Arendt and the Eichmann Controversy." *Women & Politics* 18.4 (1998) 57–79.

Robson, David. "The Threat of Contagion Can Twist Our Psychological Responses to Ordinary Interactions, Leading Us to Behave in Unexpected Ways." BBC, April 2, 2020. https://www.bbc.com/future/article/20200401-covid-19-how-fear-of-coronavirus-is-changing-our-psychology.

Rohr, Richard. *The World, the Flesh, and the Devil.* London: SPCK, 2021.

Rottman, Joshua. "Is Covid-19 Inflaming Prejudice? Our Behavioral Immune Systems Can Make Dangerous Mistakes." *Psychology Today*, June 11, 2020. https://www.psychologytoday.com/gb/blog/moral-boundaries/202006/is-covid-19-inflaming-prejudice.

Rucyahana, John. *The Bishop of Rwanda: Finding Forgiveness amidst a Pile of Bones.* Nashville: Thomas Nelson, 2008.

Rutledge, Flemming. *The Crucifixion: Understanding the Death of Jesus Christ.* Grand Rapids: Eerdmans, 2017.

Schaller M. "The Behavioural Immune System and the Psychology of Human Sociality." *Philosophical Transactions of the Royal Society of London. Series B, Biological Sciences*, 366.1583 (2011) 3418–26.

Singer, Peter. *Practical Ethics.* Cambridge: Cambridge University Press, 1979.

Southern Poverty Law Center. "Holy Hate: The Far Right's Radicalization of Religion." *Intelligence Report.* Spring Issue, 10 February 2018: https://www.splcenter.org/fighting-hate/intelligence-report/2018/holy-hate-far-right%E2%80%99s-radicalization-religion.

Stiff, Anthony J. "Keeping the Feast: The Socializing Dynamics of the Eucharist, 1 Corinthians 11:17–34, and Enabling Boundaries for Individuals with Disabilities." *Journal of Disability & Religion* 26.3 (2022) 265–79.

Strømmen, Hannah. "Christian Terror in Europe? The Bible in Anders Behring Breivik's Manifesto." *Journal of the Bible and Its Reception* 4.1 (2017) 147–69.

Swinton, John. *Becoming Friends of Time: Disability, Timefullness, and Gentle Discipleship.* Waco, TX: Baylor University Press, 2018.

———. *Raging with Compassion: Pastoral Responses to the Problem of Evil.* Grand Rapids: Eerdmans, 2007.

Thompson, Damian. "Why Liberals Turn a Blind Eye to the Global Persecution of Christians." *The Spectator*, September 2, 2019. https://www.spectator.co.uk/article/why-liberals-turn-a-blind-eye-to-the-global-persecution-of-christians.

Townsend, Mary. "The Day No One Would Say the Nazis Were Bad." *Plough*, 12 August 2022. https://www.plough.com/en/topics/community/education/the-day-no-one-would-say-the-nazis-were-bad.

The United Nations Office of Drugs and Crime. "Trafficking in Persons: Universally Defined in the UN Trafficking in Persons Protocol." https://www.unodc.org/documents/data-and-analysis/glotip/Annex_II_-_Definition_and_mandate.pdf.

Watts, Joel. "Breivik's Christ-less 'Christianity.'" *Unsettled Christianity*, July 25, 2011. https://unsettledchristianity.com/breiviks-christ-less-christianity/.

Westbrook, Adam, and Lindsay Ven Dyke. "Why Do We Let Corporations Profit from Rape Videos?" *New York Times*, April 16, 2021. https://www.nytimes.com/2021/04/16/opinion/sunday/companies-online-rape-videos.html.

White, Thomas. "What Did Hannah Arendt Really Mean by the Banality of Evil?" *Encyclopedia Britannica*, https://www.britannica.com/story/what-did-hannah-arendt-really-mean-by-the-banality-of-evil. Accessed August 4, 2022.

"Why the Pandemic Unleashed a Frenzy of Toilet Paper Buying." *Nature*, June 19, 2020. https://www.nature.com/articles/d41586–020–01836–1.

Wikipedia. "Hatred." https://en.wikipedia.org/wiki/Hatred#:~:text=Hatred%20.

Wilson, Gary. *Your Brain on Porn: Internet Pornography and the Emerging Science of Addiction*. Margate, UK: Commonwealth, 2014.

Winner, Lauren F. *The Dangers of Christian Practice*. New Haven, CT: Yale University Press, 2018.

Wright, Tom. *Following Jesus: Biblical Reflections on Discipleship*. London: SPCK, 2014.

Subject Index

Scripture Index

1 Corinthians

Ephesians

Colossians

2 Timothy

Hebrews

1 Peter

Made in the USA
Columbia, SC
05 January 2024

29915710R00086